Potpourri
AND FRAGRANT CRAFTS

Potpourri
AND FRAGRANT CRAFTS

Betsy Williams

Reader's Digest

THE READER'S DIGEST ASSOCIATION, INC.
Pleasantville, NY • Montreal

The information in this book is true and complete to the best of our knowledge.
All recommendations are made without guarantee on the part of the author or
the producer. The author and the producer disclaim any liability incurred with
the use of this information.

A READER'S DIGEST BOOK
Conceived and Produced by Elizabeth Simon Associates, ESA INC.

Director: *Elizabeth Simon*
Design Director: *Michele Italiano-Perla*
Photographer: *Tom Hopkins*
Stylist: *Deborah Kenty-Wheeler*
Illustrator: *Robert Bainbridge*

Library of Congress Cataloging in Publication Data

Williams, Betsy.
    Potpourri and fragrant crafts / Betsy Williams
            p.   cm.
    Includes bibliographical references and index.
    ISBN 0-89577-866-1
    1. Potpourris (Scented floral mixtures) 2. Decoration and
        ornament—Plant forms. I. Title
        TT899.4.W55 1996
        668'.542—dc20

Printed in USA

The Craft Room   79

Mysteriously and powerfully, our sense of smell awakens and excites the imagination. Odors slip unchallenged through the corridors of body and mind until they emerge in the hall of memory, remaining there to startle and delight us. Thanks to this stealthy magic, a transient natural fragrance may transport us from a city street into grandmother's summer garden. A single whiff can rekindle holiday memories, or enable us to relax, refreshed by an image of a placid pond or golden autumn woodland.

In this sense, potpourri might be called a mixture of memories. Making potpourri by blending fragrant substances in a way that will delight the nose and eye and stir emotions is a fascinating and rewarding art. Although the materials are simple—dried scented flowers, leaves, barks, roots, seeds, gums, resins, rinds, berries, and oils—they provide endless opportunities for exploring their aromatic powers and visual subtleties.

Clean, Crisp Scents of Today Until quite recently, natural fragrances were used primarily to mask the unpleasant odors that result from a lack of public sanitation and frequent bathing. Today, however, a new, more subtle role is emerging, as researchers investigate the effect natural fragrances play on our physiological and psychological well being. A report in the *Journal of the American Dental Association* tells how researchers at one university found that natural fragrance could reduce patients' anxiety during treatment. They sprayed small amounts of different fragrances into a treatment room as each of 42 patients underwent root canal treatment. They noted that 82 percent of these patients experienced lower levels of anxiety after inhaling certain natural fragrances.

This kind of work seems to confirm a long-held popular belief that natural fragrances have a profound effect on our minds and bodies. Crisp, clean scents have been demonstrated to refresh us mentally and physically; sweet floral bouquets soothe and relax; and the spicy aromas of cinnamon, cloves, ginger, and allspice, used so extensively in winter cooking and baking, especially during the holidays, energize us. It is not surprising that potpourris, with their natural perfumes, as well as herbal and floral crafts, are being featured more prominently in many homes.

Precious Commodities of Old The history of fragrance is the history of humankind. Many trade routes were established to buy and sell more new and different aromatic substances that were among the most precious commodities of the ancient world. On their behalf, continents were explored and mapped, cities founded and destroyed, cultures raised and ravaged, languages born and buried, and wars won and lost.

The engine of such energy was the daily use of fragrance from the most ancient times, in every civilization: China, India, Babylon, Egypt, Greece, and Rome. Scented plant materials were used in oils, creams, incense, and perfumes intended to mask the inescapable reek of daily life with minimal sanitation, heal the sick, and appease the gods. During the reign of Babylon's king Hammurabi, nearly 4,000 years ago, 30 tons of incense were burned each year in the great Temple of Bel. When the Greek physician Hippocrates built his open-walled hospital on the island of Cos, he surrounded it with beds of fragrant herbs and flowers so that the scents would aid in his patients' recovery. Ancient Egyptians and Hebrews anointed their bodies with scented oils to protect their skin from the sun and to invigorate themselves.

During the 14th and 15th centuries, great fortunes were made from the sale of orrisroot, the rhizome of the Florentine iris. Used for its violet-like fragrance as well as its ability to fix and hold other scents, orrisroot helped support Renaissance artists, musicians, and writers. In 17th-century England people so loved fragrance that they wore scented leather gloves and shoes. By the 18th century, fashionable European women had powdered fragrant herbs sprayed over their elaborate hairdos.

It was at this time that the word *potpourri* came into common use. Derived from the French, potpourri literally translates as "rotten pot." The first potpourris were made by fermenting partially dried fragrant plant material in large covered crocks until a brown paste formed. Today, potpourri describes a mixture of colorful dried flower petals, leafy herbs, and other botanicals that are mixed with spices, vegetative fixatives, and fragrant oils, and commonly used to scent a room.

SAFETY TIPS

Making potpourri involves working with fresh and dried plant material as well as fragrant oils and fixatives. The materials and equipment needed are neither dangerous to use nor hazardous to your health. By following certain guidelines, however, you can make mixing and crafting potpourri a safe and pleasant experience.

Don't attempt to make potpourri if you know or suspect that you have allergies. Plant dust is present during the blending and mixing of materials, and two basic ingredients—the highly concentrated essential oils and the fragrance oils — can trigger allergic reactions.

Avoid dripping fragrance and essential oils onto painted, varnished, or veneered surfaces. The oils are so concentrated that they could damage those surfaces.

Keep all oils, fixatives, and botanicals out of reach of children and pets; many of these materials are toxic if ingested.

Don't eat a potpourri mix, no matter how tempting it may look.

Supervise children of school age when making potpourri, and be sure to put away all materials after they are used.

Use spoons and bowls made of glass, stainless steel, pottery, or enamel when mixing blends. Wooden and plastic utensils are not recommended because they absorb the fragrance. If you have sensitive skin, wear protective gloves.

Check your local protected plants list before gathering any botanicals in the wild. Do not harvest anything on the protected list.

Don't uproot, damage, or destroy any plant when gathering fresh plant material for drying. Never take more than you need.

Don't park on the sides of major highways to gather plant material. This creates traffic hazards and is illegal in many areas.

Take a friend along for company and wear long pants and stout shoes when collecting material in the wild.

Don't pick botanicals on private property without permission.

Use caution when handling herbs. For example, wormwood (*Artemesia absinthium*) can cause severe allergic reactions in some people.

The Elements of Potpourri

$\mathcal{Potpourri}$ is a delightful, easy-to-make source of fragrance to have around your home and office. Whether you are concocting your own blend or following a recipe, you will need only three basic groups of ingredients: bulk botanicals for color, texture, and some fragrance; natural fixatives for holding, or fixing, the fragrant oils and preventing them from evaporating too quickly; and aromatic oils for strong fragrance.

Botanical blends and herbal mixes may look, feel, and smell like potpourri, but technically they are distinct because they do not contain oils or fixatives. The fragrances these blends and mixes impart come from the naturally occurring essential oils found in the plant material itself. They are quick to make and require no aging, so they can be used at once.

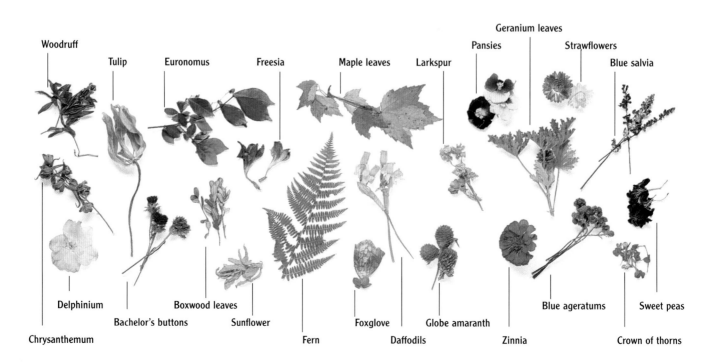

Bulk botanicals

These make up the largest group of ingredients used in blending potpourri. Botanicals encompass plant material—leaf, flower, fruit, root, bark, twig, seed, berry, cone, nut, seedpod, peel, or rind—that makes an interesting visual or scented addition to a fragrant mix. Classic potpourri recipes call mainly for rose petals, but a modern approach is to substitute the colorful dried petals of seasonal flowers, as well as the fragrant leaves and needles of herbs, shrubs, and trees. These can be successfully combined with seeds and seedpods, bits of bark, dried fruits and peels, evergreen cones, nuts and berries. If you are designing your own potpourri, try to include one or two ingredients from each of the following bulk groups.

Purple coneflower
Echinacea purpurea

Colorful leaves and blossoms
Forsythia blossoms, dogwood flowers, daffodils, hyacinths, tulips, boxwood leaves, colorful fall leaves, ferns, violets, delphinium and larkspur flowers, salvia flowers, nigella flowers, pansies, sunflower petals, pink, blue, and white ageratums, pot marigolds, zinnias, asters, globe amaranths, strawflowers, cornflowers, daisies, chrysanthemums, and foxgloves are some of the attractive possibilities. Don't overlook houseplants or office plants. Geranium flowers dry well, as do ficus leaves, crown-of-thorns flowers, and ferns.

Fragrant flowers and leaves
Three types of flowers hold their fragrance after drying: a few of the antique roses, such as Hansa and Marquise Bocella; everlasting, both pearly and sweet; and lavender. Other flowers lose fragrance as they dry but make colorful and textural additions to mixes.

Many leaves hold a strong fragrance for years. Among them are the basils, mints, bays, bee balm, lemon balm, lavender, rosemary, the thymes, lemon verbena, costmary, tansy, southernwood, sweet woodruff, scented geraniums, the sages, patchouli, eglantine roses, sweet myrtle, eucalyptus, bayberry, and sweet fern.

Lemon balm

Thyme sprigs

Sunflower petals

Bayberry

Pink geranium

White geranium

Purple basil

Chocolate mint

Sweet fern

Lemon verbena

Tansy leaves

Eucalyptus

Bay leaves

Lavender seed

Lavender sprigs

Store all dried fruits and potpourri containing dried fruit in the refrigerator or freezer during hot, humid times of the year. This prevents mealy moth infestation of the fruit.

Fruits and berries All citrus fruits dry well, either as small whole fruits, fruit slices, or cut peels. Kumquats, key limes, small lemons, and small oranges can be dried whole. Regular-size oranges, grapefruits, lemons, and limes make excellent slices and cut peels. Whole pomegranates and artichokes can be dried easily. Apple skins can be peeled off and then dried, or the apples with their skins can be cut into slices and dried. Cranberries, rose hips, barberries, blueberries, peppercorns, and the berries of bittersweet, mountain ash, and hawthorn dry well and enhance visual appeal.

Herbal seeds and spices Check your collection of seasonings or supermarket shelves for fragrant herbal seeds and whole spices, such as cinnamon, cloves, allspice, nutmeg, star anise, mace, coriander, cardamom, vanilla bean, anise seed, dill seed, fennel seed, celery seed, juniper berries, black peppercorns, and nigella seed. Unless a recipe specifically calls for powdered spices, don't use them; they can cloud a mix and destroy its visual beauty. If you need to break up woodlike whole spices, place them in a mortar and pound them with a pestle until they are partially broken up.

Freshly grated, crushed, or powdered spices have stronger and longer-lasting fragrances than store-bought ones. Buy whole seeds and spices at an herb shop or anywhere you find them being sold in bulk. (It costs less than if you purchase them at the supermarket.)

Cones, nuts, seedpods, woods, barks, and moss The hard surfaces and sculpted shapes of cones, nuts, seedpods, woods, and barks and the lacy texture of sheet moss give a visual richness to potpourri mixes. Hemlock cones and pinecones, in particular, often play a dual role in recipes because of their shape and ability to absorb and hold fragrant oils. They are used both as textural accents and as secondary fixatives.

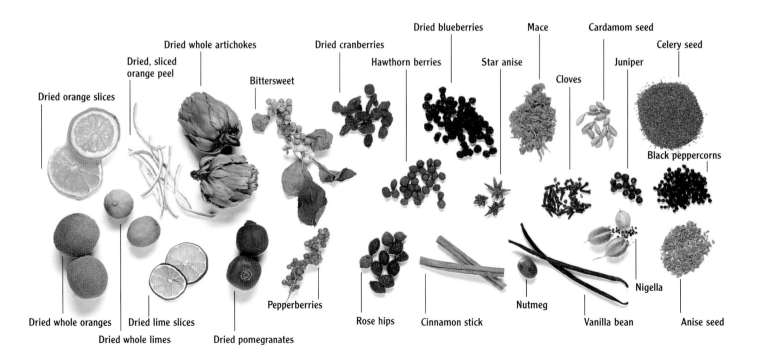

Dried orange slices
Dried whole oranges
Dried, sliced orange peel
Dried lime slices
Dried whole limes
Dried whole artichokes
Bittersweet
Dried pomegranates
Pepperberries
Dried cranberries
Hawthorn berries
Rose hips
Dried blueberries
Star anise
Cinnamon stick
Mace
Cloves
Nutmeg
Cardamom seed
Juniper
Vanilla bean
Nigella
Celery seed
Black peppercorns
Anise seed

Small cones are invaluable in creating fall and winter potpourri, garlands, tree decorations, and gifts. Hemlocks, larches, birches, and white cedars are easily available sources of small cones. Pines, cedars, spruces, and firs yield larger cones, which can be used whole or snipped and sliced into rosettes and individual scales.

Whole nuts and nutshells contribute bulk, texture, and color to mixtures. Either buy them at the supermarket or gather them in the fall as they drop from trees. Don't worry if the squirrels get to the whole nuts first; sections of shells as well as the husks of nuts, such as hickory and beech, are often just as interesting.

Fall is also a good time to look for seedpods from trees, shrubs, and flowers. Sweet gum balls, lilac, rhododendron, honesty, St. John's wort, and eucalyptus are a few that offer intriguing shapes and colors.

You can add distinctive aromas and wonderful texture to potpourri blends with curls and chips of fragrant woods, such as sandalwood, cedar, sassafras, pine, hickory, and apple. The woods act as a secondary fixative, absorbing and holding the fragrant oils.

If you live in an area where sassafras grows wild, snip off the tender tips of its branches, cut them into matchstick-size pieces, and add them to a potpourri to dry in place.

Many trees have interesting bark that makes striking visual accents. Peel bark only from fallen trees and branches, never from living trees. And if a recipe requires crushed bark, remember to weigh it before pounding it with a hammer.

Green sheet moss is valued by potpourri makers for its lacy appearance and ability to absorb fragrant oils. Tufts and small strips are excellent for decorating wreaths and twig balls. Larger pieces are useful for covering baskets. Sheet moss is available at most craft and florist shops. Before purchasing any packaged sheet moss, check that it has a rich green surface and an earthy brown back.

Supermarkets sell small bags of hickory and apple chips for flavoring barbecued meats and vegetables. Stir them into potpourris.

You should be able to find aromatic cedar curls in most pet stores, where they are sold as animal bedding. Sassafras and sandalwood are usually available at stores that sell bulk herbs, or they can be ordered from mail-order suppliers.

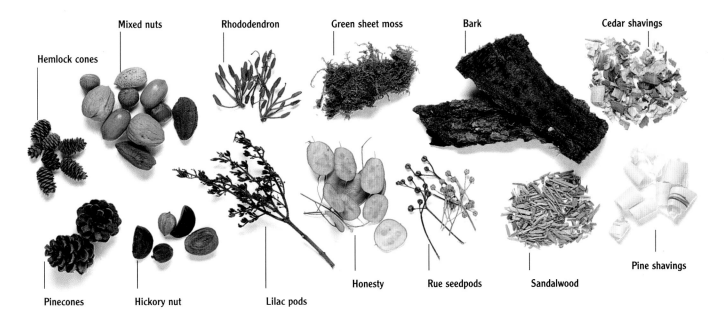

Mixed nuts

Rhododendron

Green sheet moss

Bark

Cedar shavings

Hemlock cones

Pinecones

Hickory nut

Lilac pods

Honesty

Rue seedpods

Sandalwood

Pine shavings

Natural Fixatives

Traditionally, animal extracts from musk deer, civet cats, sperm whales, and beavers were used to preserve scent. Although they are powerful fixatives, they are rarely chosen today because of environmental and ethical concerns about the methods of collection and the strong possibility of species extinction.

Botanical fixatives—renewable, widely available, and reasonably priced—have largely replaced animal-extract fixatives. The primary job of these materials is to absorb and blend the various fragrances in a potpourri, then slowly release a mature scent over time. All potpourri recipes call for at least one kind of natural (plant) fixative, some for two or three different kinds. Some expert potpourri makers feel that scents last longer and are greatly enriched by the addition of at least two fixatives.

Orrisroot

This classic and widely used fixative absorbs and retains scent longer than any other botanical fixative. It is available in chunks, granules, and powder. Orrisroot is the thick, fleshy root, or rhizome, of the Florentine iris, a delicately shaded white iris with a soft blue cast. Every three years in autumn, clumps of iris are lifted out of the ground and the largest, plumpest rhizomes removed. The smaller roots are replanted to ensure future crops. The freshly harvested roots are peeled, sliced, chopped, and spread on large trays to dry. The bone-white peeled roots dry hard as stone. Powdered orrisroot is made by pulverizing the peeled roots when they are partially dry. It takes at least three years of curing after the roots have dried for their subtle violet fragrance to age and fully develop.

Orrisroot is widely available as a powder or in cut, peeled, and dried chunks. The cut-and-dried chunks are considered by many to be the finest fixative available. The powdered form, which coats and clouds ingredients, gives a dusty look to potpourri. It is, however, a key ingredient in aromatic sachets. There can be a downside to the use of orrisroot. Some people have an allergic reaction, especially to the powdered form. Cellulose granules (ground corncob) and oakmoss are safe substitutes.

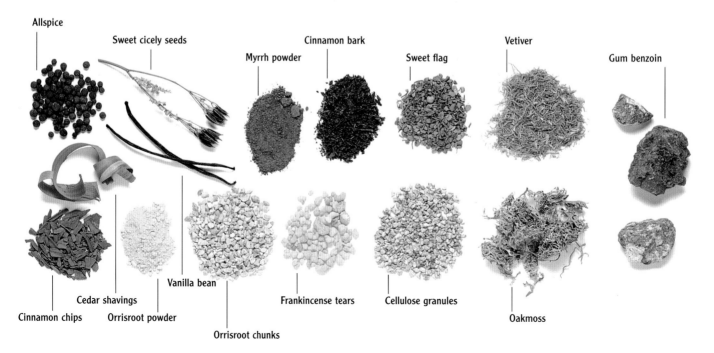

Allspice
Sweet cicely seeds
Myrrh powder
Cinnamon bark
Sweet flag
Vetiver
Gum benzoin

Cinnamon chips
Cedar shavings
Orrisroot powder
Vanilla bean
Orrisroot chunks
Frankincense tears
Cellulose granules
Oakmoss

Oakmoss This gray, lacy-looking lichen is found throughout the world's temperate zones. Sometimes called perfume lichen, or tatter lichen, oakmoss grows in clumps on branches of trees and shrubs, as well as on old wooden structures. It has the ability to fix a scent and add bulk, texture, and a sweet, earthy fragrance to potpourri mixes.

Always buy oakmoss from an herb or craft shop. Although lichens are a renewable resource, overpicking can damage their specialized growing conditions. Commercially available mosses and lichens are harvested by professional wildcrafters, who are careful not to damage the source of their income.

Cellulose granules Cellulose granules (or ground corncobs) were introduced several years ago as an inexpensive and readily available alternative to orrisroot for people with allergies. Because of their light weight and soft texture, cellulose granules require the addition of more oil than do other fixatives. A well-known Ohio potpourri maker recommends using ½ teaspoon (3 grams) of oil per 1 tablespoon (15 grams) of cellulose fiber. She also suggests mixing the oil and cellulose granules for at least 48 hours before the potpourri is made, so that the granules can completely absorb the oil.

Cellulose granules are readily available in pet stores, where they are sold as litter for rabbits, gerbils, and hamsters.

Gum benzoin The dried sap, or resin, of the gum tree native to Southeast Asia is available in powder form and in gray-brown, rocklike chunks that must be hammered into manageable pieces. Highly aromatic, gum benzoin fulfills a triple role, contributing fragrance to potpourri as well as blending and fixing the scent.

Calamus root Calamus root, or sweet flag, a fragrant rhizome, or fleshy root, is harvested from a wild marsh plant. Its sweet, fruity fragrance has made it a prized addition to mixes since biblical times. An excellent fixative, it is not as widely available as orrisroot and is much more expensive.

Vetiver This sweetly scented grass native to tropical India grows from large fibrous mats of aromatic roots. These roots, when cut and dried, impart a wonderful fragrance to potpourris, and they make a good fixative, too.

Secondary fixatives Many skilled potpourri makers recommend using more than one fixative. Secondary fixatives can supplement and enhance a fragrance by helping to hold the fragrance as well as adding subtle overtones of supporting scent. A mix of equal parts of coarsely ground hard spices, such as cinnamon bark, cloves, allspice, and nutmegs, combined with crushed frankincense and myrrh, is often used as a secondary fixative. Other botanicals valued as secondary fixatives include coriander seeds, vanilla bean, tonka bean, angelica seeds and roots, sweet cicely seeds, musk seeds, sweet woodruff, and patchouli.

If a recipe calls for crushed seeds, be sure to weigh the whole seeds first. Put the hard spices in the center of a dish towel, fold half the towel over them, then roll a rolling pin or a kitchen crushing ball (which looks and feels like a small cannonball) back and forth over them. Or pour the spices into a shallow mixing bowl, and roll the ball over them until they are crushed. If you don't have either of these useful tools, put the hard spices in the center of a dish towel, cover them with half the towel, and crush them carefully with a hammer.

Potpourri oils

Two types of oils are used to enhance the scent of potpourris—essential oils and fragrance oils.

Essential oils
Essential oils are highly concentrated aromatic oils distilled directly from plants. They are added drop by drop onto the fixative material. All are highly volatile—that is, they evaporate easily in the open air. Because they are so concentrated, essential oils can be damaging to the skin, painted and varnished surfaces, and wood veneers.

Direct light can damage essential oils; buy them in amber-colored bottles or store them in a dark cupboard. Essential oils are usually sold in ¼- or ½-oz (7- or 15-ml) bottles in craft or herb shops. The retail price tends to be higher than that of fragrance oil because so much plant material is needed to extract even a small amount of essential oil.

Fragrance oils
Although all fragrant leaves and flowers contain essential oils, it is not always easy or profitable to distill them. Fortunately, in the 1950s fragrance oils were developed in laboratories to simulate floral scents. Fragrance oils smell like the flowers and spices they are named for but are compounded in a laboratory—not distilled from plants.

In fact, most of the floral oils and some of the spice oils that are sold in herb and craft shops are synthetic. Lavender oil and most of the herb and citrus oils are distilled from the plant and, therefore, are essential oils.

The quality of a potpourri's final fragrance is directly related to the quality of the oil used when assembling the mix. Use essential oils whenever possible. When you do buy a fragrance oil, be sure to smell it first. Manufacturers use different formulas. Check several brands to find one that suits your personal aesthetic sense.

Fragrance oils

Essential oils

The ideal time for collecting fragrant plant material is on a warm, dry day just after the morning dew has evaporated, but before the sun's heat dissipates the fragrant oils in the leaves and flowers. Pick a few blossoms from a flowering shrub. Pluck some leaves from an ivy plant. Scoop up a handful of acorns or nut shells from the ground. If you grow your herbs and seasonal plant material in a garden, in planters and window boxes, or you gather botanicals in the woods and along the roadsides, you will have the beginning of a collection of plant material suitable for adding texture, visual interest, and bulk to potpourri mixes.

In addition, many common fruits and vegetables can be dried and recycled into potpourri material, including apple and citrus peels; the leafy greens of celery, carrots, and parsley; mature green beans; unused button mushrooms; and garlic cloves.

The tall, stately, and imposing Teasel, *Dipsacus fullonum* ssp. is valued most by herbalists for its golden seed heads. Although rarely used in potpourri, Teasel can be a stunning addition to winter decorations. Be sure to wear gloves when handling teasels; they can puncture the skin and cause infection.

Preparing Your Harvest

Botanicals must be prepared for use. If you have gathered cones, pods, leaves, mosses, and nuts—either from your yard or during woodland walks—treat them with heat or cold to destroy any insect life they may harbor.

To use heat on hard-shelled treasures, such as nuts, cones, and pods, spread them in a single layer on a baking sheet and put in a 150°F (66°C) oven for 2 to 3 hours. Allow them to cool before storing or using.

To treat the materials with cold, place them in a sturdy plastic bag and put into a freezer set at 0°F (-18°C) for 4 or 5 days. Freezing is also a good way to treat lichens, sheet moss, and autumn leaves that you have gathered.

Air-Drying

Although there are a number of ways to dry plant material at home, air-drying is the oldest, easiest, and most widely used method.

Basic Tools

Garden clippers

Scissors

Rubber bands

Dehydrator

Silica gel

Glass jars or plastic boxes with air-tight lids

Clean, fine sand

Air-drying flowers and herbs Harvest only the freshest-looking stems of herbs and flowers. Keep the flower heads, leaves, and stems whole, if possible, in order to preserve their fragrant oils. Bunch four to eight stems together (if the stems are thick, bunch only three or four together) and bind them with a rubber band, not string or ribbon. As the stems dry, they shrink. The rubber bands constrict with the shrinking stems and prevent them from falling to the floor. Hang the bundles upside down from a line, drying rack, or coat hanger in a warm, dim, dry spot, such as an attic or spare room, that has good air circulation. To maintain good color and form, plant material should be dried relatively quickly. The optimum temperature should consistently range between 85°F and 120°F (29°C and 49°C). Under these conditions most flowers and herbs will dry in 6 to 10 days. Flowers dried at too high a temperature, in sharply varying temperatures, or at low temperatures can lose their color and fall apart easily. Herbs, too, should be dried in consistent warmth, with temperatures never exceeding 120°F (49°C), in order to preserve their leaf color and fragrance.

Air-drying flowers, petals, and leaves To air-dry flower heads, petals, and leaves, spread them in a single layer in a flat basket or on a screen with space between each one. The faster the plant material dries, the clearer and stronger the color will be, so choose a spot that is consistently warm—between 85°F and 110°F (29°C and 43°C)—and dimly lit. During the summer, a good place to dry flower heads and petals is in the trunk of a car, where it is dark, dry, and hot. After 2 or 3 days, when the flower heads and petals are crisp-dry, store them in glass jars or plastic boxes with tight-fitting lids.

Choose only the freshest-looking stems of herbs and flowers to harvest. Keep flower heads, leaves, and stems whole in order to preserve their fragrant oils.

PLANTS, FLOWERS, AND HERBS FOR AIR-DRYING

PLANTS AND FLOWERS

Annuals

	WHAT TO PICK	WHEN TO PICK
Acroclinium	flower	fully open
Strawflower	flower	bud or first two rows of petals open
Statice	flower cluster	fully open
Statice-Pink Poker	flower stalk	full bloom
Xeranthium	flower	fully open
Ammobium	flower	fully open or in bud
Globe Amaranth	flower	flower fully developed and rounded
Orange Amaranth	flower	flower fully developed and rounded
Larkspur	flower stalk	fully open
Nigella	seed pod	as soon as fully developed
Briza Maxima	bloom stalk	as soon as fully developed
Job's Tears	seed capsules on stalk	as soon as fully developed
Broom Corn	seed head	as soon as fully developed
Celosia, Plume	plume	as soon as fully developed
Celosia, Crested	flower	as soon as fully developed
Oats	bloom stalk	as soon as fully developed
Bachelors Button	flower	just after blooming while center of flower is still tight
Foxtail Millet	bloom stalk	as soon as fully developed
Lonas, Ageratum	flower cluster	as soon as fully developed
Blue Salvia-Farinacea	budded flower stalk	full bud, just prior to bloom
White Salvia-Farinacea	budded flower stalk	full bud, just prior to bloom
Bells of Ireland	flower stalk	bottom flowers fully open
Sorghum	seed head	as soon as fully developed
Love Lies Bleeding	flowers	as soon as fully developed
Helipterum	flower	full bloom
Rhodanthe	flower	full bloom
Blue Ageratum	flower	full bloom

Biennials

	WHAT TO PICK	WHEN TO PICK
Silver Dollars, Honesty	seedpod	when outer covering is dry and papery
Onion	flower	full bloom
Foxglove	seed stalk	as soon as fully developed (poisonous)

Perennials

	WHAT TO PICK	WHEN TO PICK
German Statice	flower stalk	after flowers have gone
Sea Lavender	flower stalk	full bloom
Globe Thistle	budded flower head	full bud; before bloom
Cupid's Dart, Catanache	bud	before flower shows
Delphinium	flower	full bloom
Chinese Lantern	seed case	green or orange stage
Red Thistle	flower	full bloom
Peony	bud	tight bud, part bloom
Multiflora Rose	seed sprays	anytime
Baby's Breath	flower	full bloom
Liatris	flower stalk	full bloom
Iris	seedpod	anytime
Leeks	flower	full bloom
Hydrangea	flower heads	full bloom—pink/lime stage
Bittersweet	berry sprays	after berry covering has turned yellow; before it opens to reveal orange fruit
Roses	flower	just opening
Squirrel Tail Grass	bloom stalk	as soon as fully developed
Ornamental Onions (Alliums)	flower	full bud/full bloom

HERBS

Annuals

	WHAT TO PICK	WHEN TO PICK
Purple Basil	flower stalk	full bloom
Coriander	seed clusters	as soon as fully developed
Dill	seed head	as soon as fully developed
Anise	seed head	as soon as fully developed
Ambrosia	flower plume	full bloom
American Pennyroyal	whole plant	in fall; after bloom has faded and plant has dried in ground
Safflower	flower	full bloom

Biennial Herbs

	WHAT TO PICK	WHEN TO PICK
Angelica	seed head	as soon as fully developed
Mullein	seed stalk	as soon as fully developed
Teasel	seed head	as soon as fully developed
Caraway	seed head	as soon as fully developed

Perennial Herbs

	WHAT TO PICK	WHEN TO PICK
Silver King Artemesia	flower head	as soon as fully developed
Silver Mound Artemesia	flower and foliage	as soon as the plant flowers; cut stems to the ground
Southernwood	foliage and/or bloom	as soon as fully developed
Fennel	seed head	as soon as fully developed
Sage	leaves	anytime before mid-September
Lady's Mantle	flower	full bloom
Feverfew	flower	full bloom
Yarrow 'The Pearl'	flower	full bloom
Wormwood	flower stalk	full bloom
Rue	seedpod	as soon as fully developed
Thyme	leaves	anytime before mid-September
Sweet Woodruff	leaves	anytime before frost
Chives	flower	full bloom
Chamomile-creeping	flower	full bloom
Hops	seed cones	September; as soon as fully developed
Lavender	buds	full bud
Bee balm	flower	full bloom
Oregano	flower buds	full bud
Egyptian Onions	sets	as soon as fully developed
Lovage	seed head	as soon as fully developed
Mugwort	flowers	full bloom
Summer Fir	flowers	full bloom
Garlic, Chives	seed heads	as soon as seeds open
Hyssop	flowers	full bloom
Tansy	flower cluster	when each button is fully rounded and developed
Costmary	flower cluster	when each button is fully rounded and developed
Yellow Bedstraw	flower	full bloom
Baptisia Australis	seedpod	as soon as fully developed
Golden Yarrow	flower head	after each tiny flower has opened; head has slightly rounded appearance
Moonshine Yarrow	flower head	after each tiny flower has opened

Sprinkle a tablespoon or two of silica gel on the bottom of each storage container as extra protection from moisture. Protected from moisture and light, the flowers will hold their color for months.

Spread flower heads and petals out in a single layer in a flat basket or on a screen. The faster the plant material dries, the clearer and stronger the color will be, so choose a spot that is consistently very warm.

Hemlock · White pine · Juniper · White cedar · Arborvitae · Yew · Holly

Air-drying evergreens To dry cedar, juniper, pine, boxwood, and other evergreens, snip off 6- to 8-inch-long (15–20-cm) fresh green pieces, choosing sprays with tiny cones if possible. Gather only a small amount from each tree. Spread the tips in a single layer in a flat basket or on newspaper or screens in a warm spot, such as the top of a refrigerator or over a furnace, for a week or more until they are crisp and dry. Greens dry well in a temperature range of 70°–120°F (21°–49°C). The lacy green tips of cedar curl as they dry, changing to a soft silvery-green shade; juniper turns a gray-green; and pine needles darken and shrink a little. Boxwood, on the other hand, will stay green for months if kept out of direct sunlight.

In order to preserve their fragrant oils, try to keep the evergreen needles and stem tips whole until you are ready to use them. When it is time to add them to a potpourri, cut the needles, including the stem tips, into 1- to 1½-in (2.5–4-cm) pieces.

The peel of one medium orange makes about ½ oz (15g) of slivered dried peel. If you buy organic citrus fruit, you can use the dried slices as a garnish for food as well as a potpourri ingredient.

Air-drying citrus Most members of the citrus family air-dry well. Small fruits, such as kumquats and key limes, can be dried whole. Slices, strips of peel, and shapes cut from larger fruits can take 2 to 3 days to air-dry to total crispness in a warm, dry spot that ranges in temperature from 65°–100°F (18°–38°C). The skin and thinly sliced fruits of grapefruits, oranges, lemons, and limes, as well as the peels of tangerines, all hold their color and fragrance as they dry.

HOW TO DRY CITRUS

If you use a lot of fresh oranges and lemons in your household, it should not take you long to build up a good supply of delicate, thin curled slivers of dried peel.

Peel the remaining membrane away from the skin after you have squeezed the juice or eaten the fruit.

Cut away the pith, or inner white part of the skin, with a small, sharp knife, leaving the pieces of the outer skin intact.

Slice the skin into toothpick-size strips and lay them in a single layer on a baking sheet or in a flat basket in a warm, dry place with a temperature range of 65°–100°F (18°–38°C).

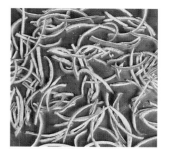

Allow 2 or 3 days for the peel to air-dry to total crispness. If you have a gas oven with a pilot light, place the sheet inside for 24 hours. When you remove the strips of peel, they will be crisp and dry.

Air-drying other fruits and vegetables Numerous other fruits and vegetables, such as strips of apple peel and apple slices, chili peppers, artichokes, cranberries, button mushrooms, pomegranates, garlic cloves, mature green beans, and rose hips can be air-dried on a baking sheet or in a flat basket kept in a warm, dry spot with a temperature range of 65°–100°F (18°–38°C). The warmer and drier the air temperature, the faster the fruits and vegetables will dehydrate.

The apple peel and mature green beans usually take 2 or 3 days to dry at 80°–120°F (27°–49°C). Other fruits and vegetables will take longer because of their size and moisture content. Artichokes, pomegranates, and cranberries, for example, can take 5 to 6 weeks to fully dry.

Desiccant Drying

Many flowers, such as chamomiles, delphiniums, and pansies, shrivel or lose their color when air-dried. However, many can be successfully dried in a desiccant, which is a drying agent that absorbs moisture from the plant material. The most commonly used are silica gel and clean sand, but white cornmeal and borax are also effective. The following flowers are a few of the many excellent selections for desiccant drying: Calendula *Calendula officinalis*; Chamomile *Chamaemelum*; Daffodil *Narcissus*; Delphinium *Delphinium*; English daisy *Bellis perennis*; Forget-me-not *Myosotis sylvatica*; Foxglove *Digitalis purpurea*; Goldenrod *Solidago odora*; Larkspur *Consolida regalis*; Lilac *Syringa vulgaris*; Mallow *Malva* spp.; Marigold *Tagetes* spp.; Nigella *Nigella damascena*; Pansy *Viola* x *wittrockiana*; Rose *Rosa* spp.; Zinnia *Zinnia elegans*.

Red Zinnias
Zinnia elegans

Sand Clean, fine sand is another excellent desiccant. It is universally available and inexpensive. In addition, it can be used in cardboard boxes without lids, and it never overdries plant material.

How to Use Sand

Place dry, undamaged flowers, slightly separated, on a 1-in (2.5-cm) layer of sand in a shallow cardboard box.
Sprinkle sand carefully over and around the flowers until they are completely covered.
Label the box with the date drying began and the type of flower, but do not cover it.
Place the box in a warm, dry spot that ranges in temperature from 65° to 100°F (18°–38°C).
Leave the dried flowers covered in sand until they are needed. As long as the storage area remains warm and dry the moisture will evaporate from the top of the box.

Silica gel Silica gel, which looks like white sand, can absorb and hold a surprising amount of moisture in its fine crystals. As a result, it dries plant material fairly quickly, often in 3 to 4 days. Marketed under various trade names, silica gel can be purchased from craft shops and florists.

Most types of packaged silica gel also contain bright blue "indicator" crystals that turn pink once they have drawn out all the water from the plants. Silica gel may be expensive, but it is a good investment because it can be used many times. To reuse them, manufacturers generally recommend spreading the moisture-filled crystals on a baking sheet or in a roasting pan and drying them slowly in a low (150°F/66°C) oven for several hours.

Pour 1 in (2.5cm) of the fine crystals into the bottom of an airtight plastic container.

Place dry, undamaged flower heads on top of the absorbent material, leaving some space between each flower.

Sprinkle silica gel over the flowers until they are completely covered. Do not dry more than one layer of flowers at a time; the weight of two layers of silica gel could damage the flowers on the bottom.

It is important to keep checking flowers covered with silica gel, because it is possible to overdry them. If that happens, the flowers become brittle and fall apart. When the flowers are dry, very gently brush away the silica gel and store them in an airtight container whose bottom has been sprinkled with a small amount of fresh silica.

Label each container with the date drying began and its contents. Since each type of flower has its own drying time, do not mix flower types in the container. Place the lid on the container and seal tightly.

Unseal the container after 3 days, and, with a soft brush, carefully remove the silica from one blossom.

Lift the flower out of the container. If the petals are stiff and papery and the base of the flower is crisply dry, remove all the flowers from the drying container.

Dehydrating

The quickest way to dry flowers such as larkspur blossoms, small spray roses, daisies, and marigolds is to place them in a food dehydrator. These are available in the kitchen sections of most department stores and are moderately priced. The appliance removes moisture from plant materials by blowing hot air over them. The best types have an adjustable thermostat and five or six stackable trays that can hold fruit slices, vegetables, leaves, or flowers. Unfortunately, the instruction book that accompanies most models usually gives drying times and temperatures for fruits and vegetables, but not flowers. Many flowers dry well in a food dehydrator set within a temperature range of 110°–130°F (43°–54°C).

Food Dehydrator

HOW TO USE A DEHYDRATOR

Place the flower heads in the trays faceup and leave some space between each one.

Dry them for 1 hour, then gently pinch each flower at the base, where the petals come together. If they are still pliable, more drying time is needed.

Check the bases every 20 minutes, because the flowers can overdry and turn brown. When they are crisply dry at the base, turn off the dehydrator and leave the dried plant material in the trays to cool.

Store the cooled flowers in an airtight plastic box whose bottom has been sprinkled with some silica gel. This process has yielded good results with larkspurs, camomiles, pansies, daisies, carnations, chrysanthemums, roses, and black-eyed susans.

Microwaving

The final results aren't in yet on this method of drying. Potpourri makers report inconsistent results.

The variables affecting this process are the oven itself and the moisture content of the plant material. Each brand of microwave oven has its own power range, and few instruction booklets give directions for drying herbs and flowers, so it is up to the user to experiment.

In most ovens, sprigs of herbs dry well by simply laying them on a turntable for a minute or less at low power. Some people cover their herbs with a paper towel, while others put paper towels under and over the sprigs. Most people report that herbs such as parsley, dill, basil, chives, and tarragon dry well, retaining both their fresh flavor and bright green color.

Flowers require different care. Most people bury them in silica gel in a nonmetallic container, then place the container in the microwave next to a glass of water to moderate the drying speed. Suggestions for the power level and length of time vary widely.

The best approach is to experiment. If you plan to dry flowers, keep a notebook handy to record the type and number of flowers, time and power setting, results, and any other variables you may introduce.

Store your botanical treasures, once they are crisp-dry, in airtight containers. Dampness in the air is quickly absorbed by naturally dried plant material and can badly damage its scent, color, and texture. Label all the storage containers so that you will know exactly what materials you have on hand when you are ready to make your potpourri.

Language of flowers

People and cultures have always assigned meanings to herbs and flowers, using the symbolism to help express themselves. During the 19th century, Victorians codified the traditional meanings of every conceivable type of plant material, investing each with symbolic importance, sometimes with quite specific intention.

One product of this effort was a series of floral dictionaries—pocket-size guides to the language of flowers for easy reference. Within their pages, the less fluent could learn that a lady carrying a small bouquet, or "tussie-mussie," of goldenrod did so to encourage the attentions of certain a gentleman, or that he could affirm his love by handing her a single tulip. Pressed flowers, potpourris, single leaves, even pictures of flowers were used to convey thoughts and emotions as surely as the spoken word.

Allspice   *Compassion*

Angelica   *Inspiration*

Artemisia   *Women's healing magic*

Baby's breath   *Everlasting love*

Bachelor's button   *Single blessedness*

Basil   *Best wishes, love*

Bay   *Glory*

Buttercups   *Cheerfulness*

Borage   *Courage*

Bee balm   *Compassion*

Blue salvia   *I think of you*

Burnet   *A merry heart*

Chamomile   *Energy in adversity*

Carnation   *Bonds of affection*

Celosia   *Immortality*

Chervil   *Sincerity*

Chives   *Usefulness*

Chrysanthemum   *Cheerfulness*

Cockscomb   *Humor*

Cinnamon   *Wisdom*

Clove   *Dignity*

Coriander   *Hidden merit*

Costmary   *Fidelity*

Daisy   *Simplicity*

Dandelion   *Oracle*

Dill   *To lull*

Fennel   *Worthy of praise*

Feverfew   *Warmth, protection*

Gardenia   *Joy, secret love*

Germander   *Joy, faithfulness*

Globe amaranth   *Unfailing affection*

Goldenrod   *Encouragement*

Hawthorn   *Hope*

Heartsease   *Happy thoughts*

Hollyhock   *Fruitfulness*

Honesty   *Money in both pockets*

Jasmine   *Amiability*

Lady's-mantle   *Comfort*

Larkspur   *Lightness, levity*

Lavender   *Devotion, cleanliness*

Lemon balm   *Pleasantry, sympathy*

Lemon verbena   *Enchantment*

Lovage   *Hidden virtues*

Marjoram   *Joy and happiness*

Mint   *Warmth of feeling*

Mugwort   *Happiness*

Myrtle   *Love, marriage*

Pansy   *Thoughts*

Parsley   *Festivity*

Peony   *Shy, bashful*

Pot marigold   *Joy*

Rose   *Beauty, love*

Rose hips   *The fruits of love*

Rosemary   *Remembrance, fidelity*

Rue   *Vision, virtue, and virginity*

Sage   *Long life, good health, and
   domestic virtue*

Scented geraniums   *Gentility*

Southernwood   *Constancy*

Strawflowers   *Friendship shall
   always be remembered*

Thyme   *Courage*

Tuberose   *A sweet voice*

Tulip   *Declaration of love*

Violet   *Modesty*

Woodruff   *Modest worth, humility*

Yarrow   *Health, war*

Zinnia   *Thoughts of absent friends*

A Medley of
Recipes

Making Potpourri

The most critical step in making potpourri, the maturing of the mix, takes patience and restraint. Although most recipes call for a minimal aging period of 3 weeks, potpourris usually develop a more complex, deeper fragrance the longer they are allowed to ripen and mellow. Subtle but important changes take place during the aging period. First, the fixatives absorb the fragrant and essential oils as well as the natural oils contained in any aromatic plant material in the mix. Then, these various scents blend with one other and mature into a rich, evocative fragrance that often is quite different and more beautiful than the individual scents.

An appropriate analogy can be made regarding the aging process of fine wines and potpourri. Some wines are meant to be drunk at once, as some potpourris are meant to be used at once. Generally, however, the wines with the fullest flavor and the potpourris with the most complex and intriguing scents are those allowed to ripen to full maturity.

Aging potpourri is a subtle process, as one herbalist learned with a mix that required large amounts of peppermint leaf. After carefully following the step-by-step directions, she allowed the mix to mature for 6 weeks. But, when she uncapped the jar, all she could smell was strongly unpleasant peppermint! Disappointed and dismayed, she recapped the jar and placed it in the back of a closet, where it stayed, forgotten, for a year. When she rediscovered the jar and opened it, a lovely fragrance wafted out. The initial disagreeable, overwhelming peppermint scent had disappeared.

CALIFORNIA MOONLIGHT

TIME INVOLVED
Making the scent • 10 minutes
Assembly • 55 minutes
Aging the mix • 2–4 weeks

RICH IN SUMPTUOUS, PROVOCATIVE FRAGRANCE, yet too delicate to handle without injury, gardenias have long been associated with moonlight romances, society orchestras, and satin ball gowns.

Botanicals

Consolida regalis	1 oz (30g) white larkspur flowers
Gomphrena globosa	½ oz (15g) white globe amaranth flowers
Umbellularia californica	1 oz (30g) California bay leaves
Oroxylum indicium	1 oz (30g) angel wings
Hibiscus	2 oz (60g) hibiscus seedpods
Arctostaphylos uva-ursi	1 oz (30g) uva-ursi
Rosa spp.	2 oz (60g) rose leaves, including the stems
Rosa spp.	6–8 white freeze-dried roses
Gardenia jasminoides	6–8 white freeze-dried gardenias

Fixatives

Iris germanica var. *florentina*	7 Tbsp (105g) cut and dried orrisroot chunks
Iris germanica var. *florentina*	2 tsp (10g) orrisroot powder

Oils
1 tsp (5ml) gardenia fragrance oil

Tools & Utensils

Small kitchen scale with a weighing basket

Set of stainless steel measuring spoons

1-gallon (3.8-l) jar with a tight-fitting lid

Eyedropper

TO CREATE THE SCENT

Place the orrisroot chunks and powder in the bottom of the glass jar.
Use an eyedropper to carefully drip the fragrance oil, a drop at a time, onto the orrisroot chunks and powder.
Cap the jar with a tight-fitting lid and shake well to thoroughly mix the oil, orrisroot chunks, and powder.

TO ASSEMBLE THE POTPOURRI

Break the white larkspur into pieces 1–1½ in (2.5–3.8cm) long.
Uncap the gallon-sized (3.8-l) jar and add the larkspur and globe amaranth flowers, bay leaves, angel wings, hibiscus pods, uva-ursi, and rose leaves to it. Try to keep the bay and rose leaves whole.
Place the freeze-dried roses and gardenias on the top of the mixed botanicals.
Recap the jar and roll it gently in your hands.
Allow the mixture to mature for 2–4 weeks. Roll the jar daily, taking care not to break the roses and gardenias. When you are ready to use the potpourri, gingerly remove the freeze-dried roses and gardenias from the top of the mixture and set them aside.
Pour the potpourri into an attractive display container and arrange the freeze-dried roses and gardenias on the top of the mixture.

MIND'S EASE

TIME INVOLVED

Making the scent • 5 minutes
Fixing the scent • at least 24 hours
Assembly • 35 minutes
Aging the mix • 2 weeks

*I*F ANY FRAGRANCE CAN TRANSFORM YOU, THIS ONE WILL, lifting your spirits, energizing your body, clearing your mind, sharpening your thinking, and reducing your stress level. To have such beneficial effects, dried aromatic plant material should be natural and fresh. The dominant fragrance in this potpourri comes directly from the dried fragrant roses grown in a Louisiana botanical garden; no rose oil was used. If you cannot grow or locate fragrant antique, or old-fashioned roses, use roses that are dried but scentless and add 20–30 drops of rose geranium oil. This oil, which is extracted from the leaves of rose geranium plants, is an essential oil. To receive the aromatherapeutic benefits of this recipe, be sure to use essential oils, not fragrance oils.

Tools & Utensils

Small kitchen scale with a weighing basket

Sharp scissors

Small glass jar with a tight-fitting lid

Eyedropper

Large glass, stainless steel, pottery, or enamel mixing bowl

Stainless steel spoon

1-gallon (3.8-l) glass jar with a tight-fitting lid

Botanicals

Rosa spp.	3 oz (90g) dried fragrant whole roses and petals
Aloysia triphylla	1 oz (30g) hard-packed lemon verbena leaves
Pogostemon cablin	¼ oz (7g) patchouli leaves
Santalum album	¼ oz (7g) yellow sandalwood chips
Lavandula angustifolia	½ oz (15g) lavender flowers

Fixatives

Evernia prunastri	¼ oz (7g) oakmoss

Oils

10 drops lavender oil
2 drops patchouli oil

TO CREATE THE SCENT

Cut the oakmoss into 1-in (2.5-cm) pieces.
Discard any twigs or stumpy clumps. Place the oakmoss in a small glass jar.
Use an eyedropper to carefully drip the lavender and patchouli oils, a drop at a time, onto the oakmoss.
Cap the jar tightly and shake vigorously to blend the oils and moss.
Allow the mixture to mature for at least 24 hours.

TO ASSEMBLE THE POTPOURRI

Pour the oiled oakmoss into a large mixing bowl.
Add all of the botanicals. Stir the mix gently and thoroughly with a stainless steel spoon, then pack it into a gallon-sized (3.8-l) glass jar and cap with a tight-fitting lid.
Allow it to mature for at least 2 weeks, shaking the jar gently each day.

OAK HILL FARM CHRISTMAS

TIME INVOLVED

Making the scent	•	15 minutes
Fixing the scent	•	at least 48 hours
Assembly	•	1 hour

CHRISTMAS CONJURES UP THE FRAGRANCE of pine, balsam, and spruce; of oranges, cinnamon, and cloves; of peppermint sticks and wood smoke; and of sweet apples and tangerines. This wonderful seasonal potpourri is made with freshly cut evergreens, gathered from the roadsides of central Indiana, and aromatic spices, visually accented with orange and apple slices. If you prepare it in early December, you will be able to enjoy its fresh, fragrant scent throughout the holidays and into the New Year.

This potpourri displays especially well in antique wooden bowls, grain measures, and cheese boxes. If you choose a wooden container, line the bottom of it with a sheet of plastic wrap to prevent the wood from absorbing the oils from the evergreens and fragrance mix.

Tools & Utensils

1-quart (.95-l) glass jar with a tight-fitting lid

Eyedropper

Large glass, stainless steel, pottery, or enamel mixing bowl or display container

Small scale with a weighing basket

Sharp kitchen scissors or garden clippers

Stainless steel spoon

Botanicals

Pinus spp.	4 large pinecones
Juniperus spp.; Pinus spp.; Abies balsamea	12 oz (336g) fresh evergreen sprigs (juniper, pine, balsam fir)
Cinnamomum cassia	1½ oz (45g) cinnamon sticks and chips
Syzygium aromaticum	½ oz (15g) whole cloves
Illicium verum	½ oz (15g) star anise
Pimenta dioica	½ oz (15g) allspice berries
Gomphrena globosa	1 oz (30g) red globe amaranth flowers
Malus spp.	8 dried apple slices
Citrus sinensis	8 dried orange slices
Punica granatum var. *nana*	3 fresh miniature pomegranates

Fixatives

Boswellia carteri	2 oz (60g) frankincense tears
Tsuga canadensis	2 oz (60g) hemlock cones

Oils

25 drops cinnamon oil

TO CREATE THE SCENT

Place the frankincense tears and hemlock cones in a quart-size (.95-l) glass jar.
Use an eyedropper to drip the cinnamon oil, a drop at a time, onto the cones.
Cap the jar with a tight-fitting lid and shake well.

TO FIX THE SCENT

Allow the oiled frankincense and hemlock cones to mature for at least 48 hours.

In the United States, fresh pomegranates are in season for about 6 weeks in late autumn and early winter. It takes at least 4 weeks to air dry a medium-size pomegranate because it contains hundreds of juicy, ruby-red seeds. However, dried pomegranates are widely available in herb and craft shops, where they are usually sold by the piece.

TO ASSEMBLE THE POTPOURRI

Snip the four large pinecones crosswise into at least 8 rosettes.
Cut the fresh evergreens into 3-in (7.6-cm) sprigs.
Put the cinnamon sticks and chips, cloves, star anise, allspice, and globe amaranth flowers into a large mixing bowl or display container.
Add the pinecone rosettes, freshly snipped greens, and oiled hemlock cones and frankincense tears to the mixing bowl or container.
Stir gently with a stainless steel spoon, drawing the smaller whole spices and flowers up through the pungent greens.
Arrange the dried apple and orange slices and the pomegranates on top.
Stir frequently during the holiday season, adding fresh greens from time to time to bolster the fragrance.

LAVENDER HOUSE ROSE GARDEN

TIME INVOLVED
Making the scent • 10 minutes
Assembly • 30 minutes

*E*ASY TO MAKE, THIS WONDERFUL POTPOURRI evokes the fragrant roses and sweet lavender that are the heart of an English cottage garden. This mix does not require aging. However, you can allow it to mature for as long as you are willing to wait for it.

Botanicals

Rosa spp.	2½ oz (75g) red roses and petals
Lavandula angustifolia	1 oz (30g) lavender

Fixatives

Iris germanica var. *florentina*	½ tsp (3g) orrisroot powder

Oils
10–20 drops rose oil

To Create the Scent
Pour the powdered orrisroot into a large mixing bowl. Mound it into the center of the bowl.

Use an eyedropper to carefully drip the rose oil, a drop at a time, onto the orrisroot powder and stir with a stainless steel spoon. (The better the quality of the rose oil, the fewer drops you will need.)

To Assemble the Potpourri
Add the roses and petals and the lavender to the mixing bowl.

Stir carefully with the stainless steel spoon to blend the botanicals with the oiled orrisroot.

Use at once or pack into a gallon-sized (3.8-l) glass jar and cap tightly.

Tools & Utensils

Set of stainless steel measuring spoons

Large glass, stainless steel, pottery, or enamel mixing bowl

Eyedropper

Stainless steel spoon

Small kitchen scale with a weighing basket

1-gallon (3.8-l) glass jar with a tight-fitting lid

CATALPA PLANTATION HERB GARDEN

TIME INVOLVED
Making the scent • 10 minutes
Assembly • 30 minutes

*S*HADES OF MAUVE PINK, LAVENDER, AND GREEN combine with lacy gray oakmoss to create a soft, feminine potpourri that captures the essence of a Georgia herb garden on a sunny late spring afternoon.

Botanicals

Rosa spp.	4 oz (120g) mauve pink roses and petals
Lavandula angustifolia	3 oz (90g) lavender flowers
Matricaria chamomilla	1½ oz (45g) German chamomile flowers
Evernia prunastri	1 oz (30g) oakmoss
Aloysia triphylla	1 oz (30g) whole lemon verbena leaves

Fixatives

Iris germanica var. *florentina*	3 Tbsp (45g) cut and dried orrisroot chunks

Oils
½ tsp (2.5ml) rose oil
½ tsp (2.5ml) lavender oil
¼ tsp (1.3ml) cinnamon oil

TO CREATE THE SCENT
Place the orrisroot chunks in a large mixing bowl.
Use an eyedropper to drip the rose, lavender, and cinnamon oils, a drop at a time, onto the orrisroot chunks.
Stir gently with a stainless steel spoon to coat the orrisroot with the oils.

TO ASSEMBLE THE POTPOURRI
Add the roses and petals and the lavender and chamomile flowers to the mixing bowl containing the oiled orrisroot.
Cut the oakmoss into ½-in (1.3-cm) pieces and discard any twigs or stumpy clump ends then add the oakmoss pieces to the bowl.
Add the lemon verbena leaves, keeping them whole if possible.
Stir the potpourri gently with the stainless steel spoon. Use at once or pack gently into a gallon-sized (3.8-l) glass jar.
Cap with a tight-fitting lid to preserve the fragrance.

Tools & Utensils

Small kitchen scale with
a weighing basket

Set of stainless steel
measuring spoons

Large glass, stainless steel,
pottery, or enamel
mixing bowl

Eyedropper

Stainless steel spoon

Sharp scissors

1-gallon (3.8-l) glass jar
with a tight-fitting lid

*C*olorful dried rose petals will enhance this lovely potpourri. According to Catalpa Plantation tradition, only mauve roses are used in the recipe.

REVIVE!

TIME INVOLVED
Making the scent • 5 minutes
Assembly • 30 minutes

*K*EEP A BAG OF THIS CLEAN-SMELLING, REFRESHINGLY SCENTED BLEND in a desk or workroom drawer. When your spirits are flagging, close your eyes and inhale deeply. Connecticut Yankees have considered the clean, crisp aromas of pine and peppermint restorative and invigorating for centuries. Traditionally, rosemary has been associated with remembrance, and thyme with strength and courage.

Botanicals

Pinus spp.	1 oz (30g) pine needles
Origanum majorana	1 oz (30g) marjoram
Rosmarinus officinalis	1 oz (30g) rosemary
Mentha piperita	1 oz (30g) peppermint
Ocimum basilicum purpureum	1 oz (30g) dark opal basil
Thymus vulgaris	1 oz (30g) thyme

Fixatives

Iris germanica var. *florentina*	1 Tbsp (15g) cut and dried orrisroot chunks

Oils

¼ tsp (1.3ml) bergamot oil

TO CREATE THE SCENT

Place the orrisroot chunks in a ½-gallon (1.9-l) glass jar.
Use an eyedropper to drip the bergamot oil, a drop at a time, onto the orrisroot. Cap the jar with a tight-fitting lid and shake gently to coat the fixative with the oil.

TO ASSEMBLE THE POTPOURRI

Use sharp scissors to snip the pine needles into 1-in (2.5-cm) pieces.
Uncap the jar containing the oiled orrisroot and add the pine needles, marjoram, rosemary, peppermint, dark opal basil, and thyme.
Cap the jar with a tight-fitting lid and shake well to blend. The mix is ready for immediate use.

*A*lthough the plum-colored leaves of dark opal basil add a dramatic visual accent to this pungent green mix, any type of green basil, such as sweet, lemon, or cinnamon, can be substituted.

Tools & Utensils

Small kitchen scale with a weighing basket

Eyedropper

Sharp scissors

Set of stainless steel measuring spoons

½-gallon (1.9-l) glass jar with a tight-fitting lid

AROHA COTTAGE CITRUS ZEST

TIME INVOLVED

Making the scent • 5 minutes
Assembly • 30 minutes
Aging the mix • 3 weeks

NEW ZEALAND IS A LAND OF BRILLIANT SUNSHINE, cheerful gardens, and friendly, energetic people. This gorgeous sun-colored citrus blend comes from Aroha Cottage in Auckland, well known for its medieval-style herb garden and afternoon teas.

Designed originally to use in "the smallest room in the house," this mix is so pretty and fragrant that it can be prominently displayed in large bowls in a kitchen or dining room or used as a welcoming fragrance by an entrance.

Botanicals

Thymus x *citriodorus*	1 oz (30g) lemon thyme leaves
Pelargonium crispum	1 oz (30g) lemon geranium leaves
Aloysia triphylla	1 oz (30g) lemon verbena leaves
Citrus limon	¾ oz (21g) small slivers and strips dried lemon peel
Citrus sinensis	¾ oz (21g) small slivers and strips dried orange peel
	1 oz (30g) dried flower heads and petals (in shades of orange, yellow, and cream)
Pimenta dioica	¼ oz (7g) allspice berries

Fixatives

Iris germanica var. *florentina*	2 oz (60g) cut and dried orrisroot chunks

Oils

3 drops lemon verbena oil
3 drops lemon thyme oil

Tools & Utensils

Small kitchen scale with a weighing basket

Set of stainless steel measuring spoons

Large glass, stainless steel, pottery, or enamel mixing bowl

Eyedropper

Stainless steel spoon

1-gallon (3.8-l) glass jar with a tight-fitting lid

TO CREATE THE SCENT

Place the orrisroot chunks in a large mixing bowl. Using an eyedropper, carefully drip the lemon verbena and lemon thyme oils, a drop at a time, onto the orrisroot.

Stir the oils and orrisroot gently together with a stainless steel spoon.

TO ASSEMBLE THE POTPOURRI

Add the lemon thyme, lemon geranium, and lemon verbena leaves, as well as the lemon and orange peels, dried flower heads and petals, and allspice berries to the oiled orrisroot.

Fold, with the stainless steel spoon, the orrisroot into the botanicals, trying not to break the flowers.

Pack the potpourri into a gallon-sized (3.8-l) glass jar and cap tightly.

Allow the mix to mature for 3 weeks, shaking the container every day to blend the orrisroot with the herbs, peels, and flowers.

PEONY

TIME INVOLVED

Assembly   •   1 hour

Aging the mix   •   3–4 weeks

EONIES ARE AMONG THE MOST ELEGANT AND FRAGRANT FLOWERS in Quebec's June gardens. Capture their brief beauty in this attractive potpourri. Gather the petals as the blooms begin to fade, then spread them on a screen to dry. Store the dried petals in an airtight glass jar until you are ready to create the blend.

Botanicals

Paeonia officinalis	4 oz (120g) peony petals
Achillea ptarmica 'The Pearl'	½ oz (15g) yarrow
Rosa spp.	1 oz (30g) rose petals, equal amounts of red and pink
Delphinium	1 oz (30g) blue or purple delphiniums

Fixatives

Iris germanica var. *florentina*	½ oz (15g) orrisroot powder

Oils

15 drops peony oil

Tools & Utensils

Small kitchen scale with a weighing basket

1-gallon (3.8-l) glass jar with a tight-fitting lid

Eyedropper

Stainless steel spoon

To Assemble the Potpourri

Place the peony petals, yarrow, and red and pink rose petals carefully in a gallon-size (3.8-l) glass jar.

Add the delphinium flowers last because they are so fragile.

Sprinkle the orrisroot powder over the botanicals.

Use an eyedropper to drip the peony oil, a drop at a time, over the mix and gently blend with a stainless steel spoon.

Cap the jar with a tight-fitting lid.

Store the finished potpourri for 3–4 weeks to allow the fragrance to mature.

CASCADE ROBE GUARD
A Mothproofing Herbal Mix

TIME INVOLVED
Assembly • 30 minutes

*F*RAGRANT CEDAR FROM THE THICK FORESTS OF THE PACIFIC NORTHWEST provides the base for this natural moth deterrent. Use this mix to protect your woolen garments from the ravages of wool-eating moths. Cedar, lavender, southernwood, and tansy all have strong, robust fragrances that, when combined with other fresh-smelling herbs, seem to act as repellents to egg-laden moths searching for a nursery for their larvae. To be effective, however, this herbal mix must be used in large quantities, and the stored clothes must be spotlessly clean and fully aired.

Botanicals

Laurus nobilis	1 oz (30g)	Mediterranean bay leaves
Juniperus virginiana	2 oz (60g)	red cedar shavings
Origanum majorana	1 oz (30g)	marjoram
Lavandula angustifolia	1 oz (30g)	lavender
Cedronella triphylla	1 oz (30g)	cedronella
Artemisia abrotanum	2 oz (60g)	southernwood
Tanacetum vulgare	1 oz (30g)	tansy

TO ASSEMBLE THE HERBAL MIX

Crumble the bay leaves into medium-size pieces over a large mixing bowl.
Add the cedar shavings, marjoram, lavender, cedronella, southernwood, and tansy to the bowl.
Mix the ingredients gently with a stainless steel spoon.

Tools & Utensils

Small kitchen scale with
a weighing basket

Large glass, stainless steel,
pottery, or enamel
mixing bowl

Stainless steel spoon

Lightweight paper bags
or old pillowcases

Stapler or needle
and thread

Airtight glass container

*T*o ensure an ample supply of Robe Guard, make twice
the amount you think you will need. Store half of it in
airtight glass jars. When it is time to change the protective
mix, you will have a fresh supply on hand. The airtight jars
keep the herbs' volatile oils from evaporating.

SIMPLY FRIENDS

TIME INVOLVED

Making the scent	•	20 minutes
Fixing the scent	•	3–4 days
Assembly	•	1 hour
Aging the mix	•	at least 6 weeks

*I*N THE VAST STATE OF TEXAS, LONG-DISTANCE FRIENDSHIPS have always been valued. A gift of potpourri can be a cheerful reminder of an especially treasured friendship (see "Language of Flowers," pages 32–33). If leaves and petals could speak, this mixture would murmur the words of Oliver Wendell Holmes: "Friendship is the breathing rose, with sweets in every fold."

Tools & Utensils

Small kitchen scale with a weighing basket

Set of stainless steel measuring spoons

Eyedropper

4 small glass jars with tight-fitting lids

Large glass, stainless steel, pottery, or enamel mixing bowl

Stainless steel spoon

Two 1-gallon (3.8-l) glass jars with tight-fitting lids

Botanicals

Celosia cristata	1 oz (30g) crested pink cockscomb
Trilisa odoratissima	½ oz (15g) deertongue
Rosa spp.	1½ oz (45g) pink rose petals and buds
Rosmarinus officinalis	1 oz (30g) rosemary
Lavandula angustifolia	⅛ oz (4g) lavender
Syzygium aromaticum	½ oz (15g) whole cloves
Cinnamomum cassia	½ oz (15g) cinnamon chips
Pimenta dioica	½ oz (15g) allspice berries
Helichrysum bracteatum	½ oz (15g) pink and white strawflowers
Limonium sinuatum	1½ oz (45g) purple and white annual statice clusters
Ammobium alatum	½ oz (15g) winged everlasting
Pelargonium graveolens	⅛ oz (4g) rose-scented geranium leaves, torn into 1-in (2.5-cm) pieces
Helipterum roseum	¼ oz (7g) pink and white acrocliniums

Fixatives

Iris germanica var. *florentina*	6 Tbsp (90g) cut and dried orrisroot chunks
Syzygium aromaticum	2 Tbsp (30g) ground cloves

Oils

½ tsp (2.5ml) lavender oil
½ tsp (2.5ml) rose geranium oil
¼ tsp (1.3ml) vanilla oil
⅛ tsp (6 ml) clove oil

TO CREATE THE SCENT

Line up four small jars with tight-fitting lids. Each jar will hold some fixative and a single oil.

- In jar 1, place 2 Tbsp (30g) orrisroot chunks. Using an eyedropper, drip the lavender oil, a drop at a time, over the orrisroot.
- In jar 2, place 2 Tbsp (30g) orrisroot chunks. Using an eyedropper, drip the rose geranium oil, a drop at a time, over the orrisroot.
- In jar 3, place 2 Tbsp (30g) orrisroot chunks. Using an eyedropper, drip the vanilla oil, a drop at a time, over the orrisroot.
- In jar 4, place the ground cloves. Using an eyedropper, drip the clove oil, a drop at a time, over the clove powder.

Cap the jars with the tight-fitting lids and shake each one vigorously to coat the fixatives with the oils.

TO FIX THE SCENT

Allow the oiled orrisroot chunks and clove powder to sit for 3–4 days.
Shake each jar briskly every day to keep the oils from settling to the bottom of the jars.

TO ASSEMBLE THE POTPOURRI

Prepare the crested pink cockscomb for weighing by snipping off most of the flat woody stem under the velvety head and discarding it.
Break the flower heads into pieces 1–1½ in (2.5–3.8cm) long. After 3 or 4 days, put the flower heads and the remaining botanicals into a large mixing bowl.
Unseal the four fixative jars and pour the oiled orrisroot and clove powder over the botanicals.
Mix gently and thoroughly with a stainless steel spoon to carefully incorporate the oiled fixatives into the plant material.
Pack the mix into 2 gallon-size (3.8-l) jars, dividing the potpourri evenly between them.
Cap each jar with a tight-fitting lid. Let this mix mature for at least 6 weeks.
Shake the jars every couple of days to keep the mix well blended.

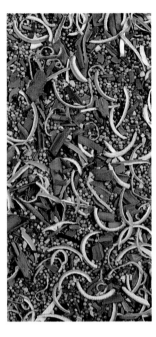

SILVER BAY CITRUS

TIME INVOLVED

Making the scent • 10 minutes
Assembly • 30 minutes
Aging the mix • at least 4 weeks

ERCHED ON THE SHORE OF PUGET SOUND IN BREMERTON, Washington, the Silver Bay herb farm concocts this stimulating potpourri year round. Especially popular during the damp winter months, the orange, lemon, and vanilla oils combine with sweet spices to create the delicious scent of candied orange slices dipped in bitter chocolate.

Botanicals

Citrus sinensis	½ oz (15g) slivered dried orange peel
Coriandrum sativum	1½ oz (45g) whole coriander seeds
Cinnamomum cassia	1 oz (30g) cinnamon chips
Syzygium aromaticum	1 Tbsp (15g) whole cloves
Vanilla planifolia	1 whole vanilla bean

Fixatives

Iris germanica var. *florentina*	2 Tbsp (30g) cut and dried orrisroot chunks

Oils

¼ tsp (1.3ml) lemon oil
¼ tsp (1.3ml) orange oil
⅛ tsp (.6ml) vanilla oil

Tools & Utensils

Small kitchen scale with a weighing basket

Set of stainless steel measuring spoons

1-quart (.95-ml) glass jar with a tight-fitting lid

Eyedropper

Sharp scissors

To Create the Scent

Place the orrisroot chunks in a quart-size (.95-l) glass jar.
Use an eyedropper to drip the lemon, orange, and vanilla oils, a drop at a time, carefully onto the fixative.
Cap the jar with a tight-fitting lid and shake well to make sure the orrisroot chunks are well coated with the fragrant oils.

To Assemble the Potpourri

Uncap the jar containing the oiled orrisroot and add the slivered orange peel, coriander seeds, cinnamon chips, and cloves.
Cut the vanilla bean into ½-in (1.3-cm) pieces and add to the jar.
Recap the jar tightly and shake vigorously to blend.
Allow the mixture to mature for at least 4 weeks, shaking the jar daily.

MOTHER'S HERBS: An Herbal Mix

TIME INVOLVED
Assembly • 45 minutes

*I*N VICTORIAN BOSTON, A STRONG SENSE OF FAMILY, with mother and father at the revered center, gave birth to this delicately scented, visually complex mix composed of herbs and herbal flowers. Using the meanings of flowers (see "Language of Flowers", pages 32–33) as their inspiration, Victorian children combined symbolic meanings to express endearment for their mothers.

It is not always easy to tell your mother how you feel about her, so why not let the language of flowers help you, too. Mix a batch of this recipe and package it in a clear glass box or other decorative container. Include a card listing the herbs and flowers used, along with their meanings.

Tools & Utensils

Small kitchen scale with
a weighing basket

1 mixing container 2–3
gallons (7.6–11.4l) in size,
with a tight-fitting lid,
a sturdy cardboard, tin, or
plastic box, or a
medium-sized
heavyweight plastic bag

Sharp scissors

Stainless steel spoon

Botanicals

Dianthus caryophyllus	½ oz (15g) carnations
Gomphrena globosa	½ oz (15g) globe amaranth flowers
Salvia farinacea	1 oz (30g) blue salvia
Chrysanthemum parthenium	½ oz (15g) feverfew
Buxus sempervirens	1 oz (30g) boxwood leaves
Thymus vulgaris	¼ oz (7g) thyme
Consolida regalis	¼ oz (7g) larkspur
Artemisia ludoviciana 'Silver King'	½ oz (15g) artemisia
Mniumhoenum	¼ oz (7g) moss
Lavandula angustifolia	1 oz (30g) lavender
Origanum majorana	¼ oz (7g) marjoram
Rosa spp.	¼ oz (7g) roses
Crataegus laevigata	½ oz (15g) hawthorn
Viola tricolor	12–15 heartsease

TO ASSEMBLE THE HERBAL MIX

Snap the dried carnation, globe amaranth, blue salvia, and feverfew flowers from their stems and put them into the mixing container.
Strip the boxwood leaves from their stems and add them to the container.
Snip the thyme stems, larkspur stalks, and artemisia into pieces 1–1½ in (2.5–3.8cm) long and pour them into the container.
Pull the moss into 1-in (2.5-cm) wisps and add them to the mix.
Add the lavender, marjoram, roses, and hawthorn to the container.
Blend the mix very gently with a stainless steel spoon, trying to keep the pieces whole. For immediate use, pour the mix in a decorative container and carefully arrange the heartsease on the top of the display.

*S*tore any leftover mix tightly covered in the mixing container. It will keep in a warm, dry place for several months. If you choose a cardboard box or plastic bag for your mixing and storage container, put the herbs in a frost-free refrigerator or freezer to prevent insect infestation that could occur during hot, humid weather.

LUST

TIME INVOLVED

Making the scent	•	5 minutes
Assembly	•	45 minutes
Aging the mix	•	2–4 weeks

ISPLAY THIS RICH, COMPLEX PENNSYLVANIA-born potpourri around Valentine's Day; top it with three or four whole dried, dark red flowers. Heighten its romance with lustrous burgundy and ruby velvets, richly cut glass and candles, and creamy satins and damasks.

Botanicals

Pogostemon cablin	1½ oz (45g) patchouli leaves
Cinnamomum cassia	2 oz (60g) cinnamon chips
Apium graveolens	2 oz (60g) celery leaf flakes
Trilisa odoratissima	1½ oz (45g) deertongue
Hibiscus sabdariffa	2 oz (60g) whole hibiscus flowers
Aframomium melegueta	1½ oz (45g) grains of paradise
Carthamus tinctorius	1½ oz (45g) whole safflower heads
Papaver rhoeas	1½ oz (45g) whole red poppy flowers
Paeonia officinalis	1½ oz (45g) peony flowers
Pterocarpus santalinus	1½ oz (45g) red sandalwood
Cymbopogon citratus	1½ oz (45g) lemongrass
Celosia cristata	1½ oz (45g) red cockscomb
Mentha piperita	1 oz (30g) peppermint

Fixatives

Iris germanica var. *florentina*	3 oz (90g) cut and dried orrisroot chunks

Oils

½ tsp (2.5ml) cinnamon oil
½ tsp (2.5ml) vanilla oil
½ tsp (2.5ml) musk oil

Tools & Utensils

Small kitchen scale with
a weighing basket

Set of stainless steel
measuring spoons

Large glass, stainless steel,
pottery, or enamel
mixing bowl

Eyedropper

Stainless steel spoon

1-gallon (3.8-l) glass jar
with a tight-fitting lid

To Create the Scent

Place the orrisroot chunks in the bottom of a large mixing bowl. Using an eyedropper, drip the cinnamon, vanilla, and musk oils, a drop at a time, over the orrisroot and stir gently with a stainless steel spoon until the orrisroot chunks are well coated with the oils.

To Assemble the Potpourri

Place the patchouli leaves, cinnamon chips, celery leaf flakes, deertongue, hibiscus flowers, grains of paradise, safflower heads, red poppy and peony flowers, red sandalwood, lemongrass, red cockscomb, and peppermint in the bowl with the oiled orrisroot and mix thoroughly but gently with the stainless steel spoon. Try to keep the leaves and flowers whole.

Pack the mix into a gallon-sized (3.8-l) glass jar and cap with a tight-fitting lid until you are ready to use.

Allow the potpourri to mature for 2–4 weeks.

HOLIDAY GREENS

TIME INVOLVED
Making the scent • 10 minutes
Assembly • 30 minutes
Aging the mix • 3–4 days

*T*HE TANGY AROMA OF THIS CHESAPEAKE BAY, MARYLAND, potpourri comes from the mingling of the freshly cut greens with the fragrant holiday spices and the orange oil. The mix will stay fragrant even after the greens are dried; just stir it every once in a while with your fingers.

Botanicals

Pinus spp.; Juniperus spp.; Abies balsamea; Cedrus spp.	8 oz (225g) fresh evergreens (pine, juniper, balsam fir, cedar)
Cinnamomum cassia	12 cinnamon sticks 3-in (7.6-cm) in length
Pimenta dioica	½ oz (15g) allspice berries
Syzygium aromaticum	½ oz (15g) whole cloves
Citrus spp.	2½ oz (75g) dried citrus peels (orange, lemon, lime, grapefruit, tangerine)
Myristica fragrans	2 whole nutmegs
Rosa spp.	4–5 sprigs of multiflora rose hips
Rhus glabra	4–5 clusters of red sumac berries

Oils
10 drops cinnamon oil
10 drops orange oil
10 drops pine, balsam, or cedar oil

Tools & Utensils

Sharp garden clippers

Small kitchen scale with a weighing basket

Large glass, stainless steel, pottery, or enamel mixing bowl

Eyedropper

Stainless steel spoon

Nutmeg grater

Heavy-gauge 2-gallon (7.6-l) plastic bag

Twist-tie or rubber band

TO CREATE THE SCENT
Use sharp garden clippers to cut the different kinds of evergreens into pieces 1–2 in (2.5–5cm) long, including the stems. Put the pieces into a mixing bowl.
Use an eyedropper to drip the cinnamon, orange, and evergreen oils, a drop at a time, onto the greens, then mix well with a stainless steel spoon.

TO ASSEMBLE THE POTPOURRI
Break each cinnamon stick in half and place them on the greens.
Add the allspice berries, cloves, and citrus peels to the greens and then grate the whole nutmegs into the bowl.
Mix all these ingredients together with the stainless steel spoon, then pack them into a heavy-gauge 2-gallon (7.6-l) plastic bag.
Tie the bag tightly and allow the mix to mature for only 3 or 4 days. If you let this mix sit in a sealed plastic bag for a longer time, the moisture in the fresh greens could cause the potpourri to decay.
Pour the mix into decorative containers and top with sprigs of multiflora rose hips and clusters of red sumac berries.

NOVEMBER ON THE NATIONAL ROAD

TIME INVOLVED

Making the scent	•	10 minutes
Fixing the scent	•	at least 48 hours
Assembly	•	45 minutes
Aging the mix	•	1 week

To capture a bit of November indoors, choose a sunny, dry day in the late fall to head off into the leafless woods to gather the brown remains of the year's forest harvest: acorns and acorn caps, hickory or other nut shells, sweet gum balls, and small cones. Add handfuls of mahogany-red rose hips, slate-blue juniper berries, and the tips of boxwood, fir, and pine to your collection.

Botanicals

Pinus spp.; Buxus spp.; Juniperus communis; Libocedrus; Abies balsamea	3½ oz (100g) mix of dried evergreen tips, needles, and sprigs (pine needles, boxwood tips, juniper sprigs and berries, incense cedar, balsam needles and tips)
Juniperus communis	1 oz (30g) juniper berries
Quercus robur	1½ oz (45g) acorns and acorn cups
Ternstroemia spp.	½ oz (15g) tilia star flowers
Tsuga spp. (or Juniperus spp.; Cedrus spp.; Abies balsamea)	1 oz (30g) hemlock or other small evergreen cones (juniper, cedar, balsam fir)
Carya ovata	1½ oz (45g) hickory nut shells
Gomphrena globosa	½ oz (15g) white or pink globe amaranth flowers
Rosa spp.	3½ oz (100g) rose hips
Liquidambar styraciflua	1 oz (30g) sweet gum balls

Fixatives

Zea mays	4 Tbsp (60g) cellulose granules (ground corncobs)

Oils

25 drops pine oil

15 drops spruce oil

10 drops vanilla oil

Tools & Utensils

Small kitchen scale with a weighing basket

Set of stainless steel measuring spoons

Small glass jar with a tight-fitting lid

Eyedropper

Sharp garden scissors or small garden clippers

1-gallon (3.8-l) glass jar with a tight-fitting lid

To Create the Scent

Pour the cellulose granules into a small glass jar.

Use an eyedropper to drip the pine, spruce, and vanilla oils, a drop at a time, onto the cellulose.

Cap the jar with a tight-fitting lid and shake vigorously to completely mix the oils and cellulose.

To Fix the Scent

Allow the mix to mature for at least 48 hours.

Shake the jar gently each day.

To Assemble the Potpourri

Snip the dried evergreen tips and sprigs and pine needles into pieces 1–2 in (2.5–5cm) long.

Place them along with the balsam needles in a 1–gallon (3.8-l) glass jar.

Add the juniper berries, acorns and acorn cups, tilia star flowers, hemlock cones, hickory nut shells, globe amaranth flowers, rose hips, sweet gum balls, and the oiled cellulose granules to the jar.

Cap the jar tightly and gently roll it in your hands. Try to distribute the oiled cellulose evenly throughout the mix.

Shake the jar carefully each day for a week or until you are ready to use it.

*N*estled on the edge of a once-abandoned section of the National Road in the crossroads village of Thornville, Ohio, sits the Herb 'n' Ewe herb farm. Its owners create this fascinating potpourri each fall, gathering ingredients from the mixed woodlands that border their property.

The National Road was the first federally funded highway in the United States. Commissioned in 1808 by Thomas Jefferson, it was to link Washington, D.C., and the frontier on the banks of the Mississippi River. Thousands of families traveled over the road, across streams and mountains, and through verdant woods and forests packed with native oak and nut trees. With them they brought their herds, flocks, seeds, and plant cuttings. The descendants of the settlers and their baggage thrive along the road today.

Eclipsed by the advent of the railroad, the highway fell into disrepair until the country's love affair with the automobile began. In the early 1930s the road was paved and renamed U.S. Route 40. It still exists, modestly making its way beside railroad tracks and super-highways from the banks of the Potomac River to St. Louis, Missouri.

PENNYROYAL ROSE

TIME INVOLVED

Making the scent • 10 minutes
Assembly • 30 minutes
Aging the mix • at least 4 weeks

*T*HIS SPICY ROSE BLEND IS AS PLEASING IN THE hot, humid summers of Queensland, Austalia, as it is in cold, blustery winters. If possible, combine naturally fragrant rose petals with the finest rose oil available. Your reward will be an aroma that stays intoxicatingly beautiful for many months.

Botanicals

Coriandrum sativum	2¼ oz (70g) coriander seeds
Cinnamomum zeylanicum	1¼ oz (40g) cinnamon stick
Syzygium aromaticum	1½ oz (45g) whole cloves
Rosa spp.	4½ oz (135g) rose petals
Lavandula angustifolia	1¾ oz (50g) lavender
Pogostemon cablin	1½ oz (45g) patchouli leaves

Fixatives

Evernia prunastri	¾ oz (21g) oakmoss

Oils

8–12 drops rose oil
2 drops patchouli oil

TO CREATE THE SCENT

Snip the oakmoss into small lacy pieces.
Discard any twigs or stumpy clump ends.
Put the oakmoss into a gallon-sized (3.8-l) glass jar.
Use an eyedropper to carefully drip the rose and patchouli oils, a drop at a time, over the oakmoss.

TO ASSEMBLE THE POTPOURRI

Crush the coriander seeds, cinnamon stick, and whole cloves to release their volatile oils.
Pour the crushed spices into the jar containing the oiled oakmoss.
Add the rose petals, lavender, and patchouli leaves.
Cap the jar with a tight-fitting lid, give it a brisk shake, and allow the mix to mature for at least 3 weeks.
Shake the jar occasionally to keep the botanicals blended.
Add more oils at the end of the initial aging period for a stronger fragrance.
Recap the jar and age for another week.

Tools & Utensils

Small kitchen scale with a weighing basket

Sharp scissors

1-gallon (3.8-l) glass jar with a tight-fitting lid

Eyedropper

Mortar and pestle, meat mallet, or hammer

*U*se any color rose petals: A mixture of reds and pinks will produce a rich Victorian feeling; white will accentuate the blue lavender and gray moss; and yellow will create a cheerful, sunny appearance.

VANCOUVER'S SUMMER SONG

TIME INVOLVED

Making the scent • 5 minutes
Fixing the scent • at least 48 hours
Assembly • 45 minutes
Aging the mix • 4–6 weeks

THE SOOTHING FRAGRANCE OF THIS PRETTY BLEND captures the distinctive essence of a late June herb garden on Vancouver Island.

Botanicals

Pimenta dioica	1½ oz (45g) allspice berries
Rosa spp.	2 oz (60g) rose petals
Consolida regalis	¾ oz (21g) pink larkspur flowers
Buxus sempervirens	1½ oz (45g) boxwood leaves and sprigs
Achillea ptarmica 'The Pearl'	1 oz (30g) yarrow
Thymus spp.	½ oz (15g) thyme sprigs
Chamaemelum nobile	½ oz (15g) whole Roman chamomile flowers
Rosa spp.	1 oz (30g) whole dried pink and red roses

Fixatives

Iris germanica var. *florentina*	1½ Tbsp (20g) cut and dried orrisroot chunks

Oils

10 drops rose geranium oil
2 drops sandalwood oil
1 drop rose oil
1 drop musk oil
3 drops tangerine or orange oil

Tools & Utensils

Set of stainless steel measuring spoons

Small glass jar with a tight-fitting lid

Eyedropper

Small kitchen scale with a weighing basket

Large glass, stainless steel, pottery, or enamel mixing bowl

Stainless steel spoon

1-gallon (3.8-l) glass jar with a tight-fitting lid

TO CREATE THE SCENT

Place the orrisroot chunks in a small glass jar. Use an eyedropper to carefully drip the oils, a drop at a time, onto the orrisroot.
Cap the jar tightly and shake vigorously to coat the fixative with the oils.

TO FIX THE SCENT

Allow the oiled orrisroot to mature for at least 48 hours.

TO ASSEMBLE THE POTPOURRI

Put all the botanicals, except for the whole roses, into a mixing bowl.
Pour the scented orrisroot into the bowl and mix with a stainless steel spoon.
Pack the mix into a gallon-sized (3.8-l) glass jar and cap with a tight-fitting lid. Very gently rock the jar back and forth in your hands. Try to keep the larkspur, chamomile, and the yarrow flowers whole.
Allow the mix to mature for 4–6 weeks, gently rocking the jar every couple of days to blend the oiled orrisroot with the botanicals. When you are ready to display the potpourri, arrange the whole roses on top of the blend.

CHRYSANTHEMUM FESTIVAL

TIME INVOLVED

Making the scent • 5 minutes
Assembly • 45 minutes
Aging the mix • 3–4 weeks

THE JAPANESE LOVE OF FLOWERS IS CELEBRATED ANNUALLY on September 9 with the Chrysanthemum Festival. It is an exciting day, when people construct life-size figures out of wire and bamboo in the shapes of samurais and princesses and cover them with a variety of colorful chrysanthemum flowers. Many Japanese follow the ancient customs of drinking chrysanthemum tea, bathing in chrysanthemum essence, and sleeping with chrysanthemum pillows—a tradition that originated in China centuries ago. Enjoy this aromatic potpourri any day of the year, or join in the celebration in September.

Tools & Utensils

Small kitchen scale with a weighing basket

Set of stainless steel measuring spoons

Small dish

Eyedropper

1-quart (.95-l) jar with a tight-fitting lid

Mortar and pestle or meat mallet

Botanicals

Chrysanthemum spp.	1½ oz (45g) colorful chrysanthemum flower heads and petals
Chrysanthemum spp.	½ oz (15g) green chrysanthemum leaves in various sizes
Mentha piperita	1 oz (30g) peppermint
Tanacetum vulgare	2 Tbsp (30g) tansy leaves
Thymus spp.	3 Tbsp (50g) thyme leaves, stems, and flowers
Coriandrum sativum	¾ oz (21g) coriander seeds
Alchemilla vulgaris	½ oz (15g) lady's-mantle flowers

Fixatives

Iris germanica var. *florentina*	2 tsp (30g) cut and dried orrisroot chunks

Oils

4 drops ylang-ylang oil

TO CREATE THE SCENT

Place the orrisroot chunks in a small dish. Using an eyedropper, drip the ylang-ylang oil, a drop at a time, over the orrisroot.

TO ASSEMBLE THE POTPOURRI

Place the chrysanthemum flower heads and petals in a quart-size (95-1) glass jar.

Add the peppermint, tansy, and thyme.

Crush the coriander with a mortar and pestle or a meat mallet. Add to the jar.

Sprinkle the oiled orrisroot chunks over the botanicals and cap the jar with a tight-fitting lid. Gently rock the jar to mix the ingredients.

Allow the potpourri to mature for 3–4 weeks, shaking the jar gently each day to ensure that the orrisroot blends well with the botanicals.

Pour the botanicals into a display container and arrange the lady's-mantle flowers on top.

LAST ROSE OF SUMMER

TIME INVOLVED

Making the scent • 10 minutes
Fixing the scent • 20 minutes
Assembly • 30 minutes
Aging the mix • 7 days

*I*N THE WILLAMETTE VALLEY OF OREGON, roses, camellias, and primroses grow with wild abandon, rosemaries become hardy shrubs, and lavenders burst with unusually fragrant oils. Evergreens abound, but during the rainy winter, the bare oaks are festooned with lacy gray moss. This type of moss is not used as a fixative. The oakmoss fixative called for here, however, also serves as an important visual element. Its lacy gray clumps intensify the deep red of the rose petals and the lime-green of the uva-ursi leaf.

Tools & Utensils

Sharp scissors

Small kitchen scale with a weighing basket

Set of stainless steel measuring spoons

Glass, stainless steel, pottery, or enamel mixing bowl

Eyedropper

Stainless steel spoon

1-gallon (3.8-l) glass jar with a tight-fitting lid

Botanicals

Abies balsamea	2 oz (60g) balsam fir needles
Rosa spp.	1½ oz (45g) red rosebuds and petals
Arctosaphylos uva-ursi	½ oz (15g) bearberry
Tsuga spp.; Juniperus spp.; Cedrus spp.; Abies balsamea	½ oz (15g) assorted small evergreen cones (hemlock, juniper, cedar, balsam fir)
Rosmarinus officinalis	1 oz (30g) rosemary

Fixatives

Evernia prunastri	¾ oz (21g) oakmoss

Oils

1 Tbsp (15ml) sandalwood oil
2 Tbsp (30ml) rose oil

TO CREATE THE SCENT

Snip the oakmoss into pieces ¼–½ in (6–13mm) in size. Discard any twigs or stumpy clump ends.

TO FIX THE SCENT

Put the cut oakmoss into a large mixing bowl. Using an eyedropper, carefully drip the sandalwood and rose oils, a drop at a time, onto the moss.
Stir with a stainless steel spoon to blend the moss and oils together. Allow the mix to sit for 20 minutes.

TO ASSEMBLE THE POTPOURRI

Add the balsam fir needles, rosebuds and petals, bearberries, evergreen cones, and rosemary to the mixing bowl, then stir gently with the stainless steel spoon to blend them with the oiled oakmoss.
Pack the mix into a gallon-size (3.8-l) glass jar and cap with a tight-fitting lid. Allow it to mature for 7 days, shaking the jar gently each day.

HAPPY VALLEY EVENING SONG

TIME INVOLVED
Making the scent • 5 minutes
Assembly • 45 minutes

As DUSK CREEPS OVER VANCOUVER ISLAND, the flowers and leaves within its fragrant gardens fill the air with their richly textured scents. This potpourri's sweet, weighty perfume will remind you of those heady smells of descending night.

Botanicals

Lavandula angustifolia	1 oz (30g) lavender flowers
Pelargonium graveolens	½ oz (15g) scented geranium leaves (preferably rose-scented)
Consolida regalis	⅛ (4g) blue larkspur flowers
Hydrangea macrophylla, Philadelphus, Gomphrena globosa	1 oz (30g) cream-colored flower petals or heads (hydrangea, mock orange blossoms, or globe amaranth)
Xeranthemum annuum	¼ oz (7g) lavender everlastings
Rosa spp.	2 oz (60g) mauve rosebuds
Origanum marjorana	1 oz (30g) marjoram
Syzygium aromaticum	⅛ oz (4g) whole cloves

Fixatives

Iris germanica var. *florentina*	½ oz (15g) cut and dried orrisroot chunks

Oils

10 drops lavender oil
5 drops ylang-ylang oil

Tools & Utensils

Small kitchen scale with a weighing basket

Small glass jar with tight-fitting lid

Eyedropper

1-gallon (3.8-l) glass jar with a tight fitting lid

To Create the Scent

Place the orrisroot chunks in a small glass jar.
Use an eyedropper to carefully drip the lavender and ylang-ylang oils, a drop at a time, onto the orrisroot.
Cap the jar with a tight-fitting lid and shake well to blend.

To Assemble the Potpourri

Place the lavender flowers, geranium leaves, larkspur flowers, cream-colored flower petals, everlastings, rosebuds, marjoram, and cloves in a gallon-size (3.8-l) glass jar. Try to keep the leaves and petals whole.
Add the oiled fixative.
Cap the jar with a tight-fitting lid and and shake gently.

HALLOWEEN HERBS: A Botanical Blend

TIME INVOLVED
Assembly • 30 minutes

$\mathcal{T}$HIS MIX WAS CONCOCTED IN SALEM, MASSACHUSETTS, home of the 17th-century Puritans, especially for this night of ghosts, goblins, and spirits both good and evil. This powerful assembly of plants and herbs was relied upon by generations of witches and sorcerers to work spells and protect their users from unwelcome forces.

The seedpod of honesty, regarded as a symbol of the moon under which witches dance, also protects against enchantment by virtue of its silver hue, the color of purity; rue, called the herb of grace, is a favorite of witches, as it protects against magic spells; sage, said to summon rain, also is used in charms as an instrument of both love and revenge; dill, however, is shunned by all witches, for it nullifies their desires; and, most famously, garlic is repugnant to witches, demons, and vampires.

Tools & Utensils

Small kitchen scale with a weighing basket

Large wooden or pottery display container

Botanicals

Anethum graveolens	½ oz (15g) dill heads
Foeniculum vulgare	½ oz (15g) fennel heads
Quercus robur	½ oz (15g) oak leaves
Salvia officinalis	½ oz (15g) sage leaves
Artemisia vulgaris	½ oz (15g) mugwort
Ruta graveolens	½ oz (15g) rue pods
Achillea filipendulina	½ oz (15g) golden yarrow heads
Allium sativum	1 oz (30g) garlic cloves
Lunaria annua	½ oz (15g) honesty, or money plant, sprigs

To Assemble the Potpourri

Crush, with your fingers, the dill, fennel, oak leaves, sage, mugwort, rue pods, yarrow, and garlic before placing them in a large display container.
Strip the copper-colored coverings from the honesty seedpods if they haven't fallen off naturally.
Add the seedpods to the display container.

$\mathcal{T}$he essential oil of rue, found in the leaf, stem, and seedpod, can cause an allergic skin reaction when handled during the heat of summer. If you intend to collect rue pods, wait until evening temperatures have cooled to about 50°F (10°C).

FROM A CALIFORNIA GARDEN

TIME INVOLVED

Making the scent	•	5 minutes
Fixing the scent	•	at least 3 weeks
Assembly	•	1 hour

*A*LTHOUGH FRAGRANCE IS AT THE HEART OF EVERY POTPOURRI, its appearance, determined by the color and texture of its materials, can enhance its impact. Create a visually striking potpourri by layering alternate bands of colorful flower heads and fragrant leaves in a clear glass apothecary bottle, antique canning jar, or other lidded, decorative clear glass container. Choose ingredients in strongly contrasting colors and shapes, or design a jar using botanicals in varying shades of one color and in contrasting textures. This potpourri can be used whenever you are ready to enjoy its fragrance; no aging is required. Just gently shake the jar and remove the lid.

Tools & Utensils

Small kitchen scale with a weighing basket

½-pint (.23-l) glass jar with a tight-fitting lid

Eyedropper

18 small plastic containers or dishes

Lidded decorative clear glass container

Large pestle or tall, narrow spray can

Botanicals

Aloysia triphylla	⅛ oz (4g) lemon verbena leaves
Helianthus annuus	⅛ oz (4g) sunflower petals
Gomphrena globosa	½ oz (15g) pink globe amaranth flowers
Lavandula angustifolia	½ oz (15g) lavender buds
Rosa spp.	½ oz (15g) rosebuds
Hydrangea macrophylla	⅛ oz (4g) hydrangea florets
Consolida regalis	⅛ oz (4g) purple larkspur flowers
Allium sphaerocephalon	⅛ oz (4g) drumstick allium heads

Fixatives

Iris germanica var. *florentina*	2 oz (60g) cut and dried orrisroot chunks

Oils

6 drops lavender oil
6 drops rose oil

To Create the Scent

Place the orrisroot chunks in a ½-pint (.23-l) glass jar. Using an eyedropper, drip the lavender and rose oils, a drop at a time, onto the orrisroot.
Cap the jar with a tight-fitting lid and shake vigorously to coat the orrisroot with the fragrant oils.

To Fix the Scent

Allow this mixture to mature for at least 3 weeks. Shake the jar each day.

To Assemble the Potpourri

Place the lemon verbena leaves, sunflower petals, globe amaranth flowers, lavender buds, rosebuds, hydrangea florets, larkspur flowers, and allium heads in individual small plastic containers.
Study the flowers and herbs you have chosen, before you begin filling the glass display jar.
Observe their shapes, colors and textures so that you can arrange them in visually appealing layers. Each flower or herb should occupy about 1 in (2.5cm) of the display jar.
Create the pattern shown here by placing a 1-in (2.5-cm) layer of lemon verbena on the bottom of a decorative clear glass jar. Gently tamp it into place with the base of a large pestle or a tall, narrow spray can. Then sprinkle a small amount of the oiled orrisroot over the center of the layer. Gently press each succeeding layer (described below) into place in the same manner and scatter the oiled orrisroot over every two or three layers.

If you prefer a stronger scent, add more oil and let the mix mature for another week. Continue to shake the jar daily.

Add a ½-in (1.3-cm) layer of sunflower petals, followed by a 1-in (2.5-cm) layer of globe amaranth flowers, a 1-in (2.5-cm) layer of lavender buds, and a 1-in (2.5-cm) layer of rosebuds. Top these off with separate 1-in (2.5-cm) layers of hydrangea, larkspur, and drumstick allium.
Drip a few more drops of the scented oils into the center of the top layer if you wish, then cap the decorative jar with a lid.

LONG CREEK HOLIDAY GREENS
A Botanical Blend

TIME INVOLVED

Assembly • 1 hour

Aging the mix • 1 week

ROM THE DEEP WOODS OF ARKANSAS'S OZARK MOUNTAINS, this earthy and richly resinous mixture springs from the very heart and soul of ancient winter celebrations. Package it in brown paper bags tied with green twine or a burlap ribbon and lavish it on friends. Its fragrance is meant to be shared and enjoyed by everyone during the dark of winter.

Tools & Utensils

Small kitchen scale with a weighing basket

Pruning shears

Paper bag

Very large container (plastic box, stainless steel bowl, cardboard carton)

Botanicals

Picea abies; Juniperus communis; Abies balsamea; Pinus spp.; Juniperus virginiana Pinus spp.; Picea spp.; Tsuga canadensis; Betula spp.	8 oz (225g) fresh evergreen tips (spruce, juniper, balsam, pine, red cedar) 1 oz (30g) assorted fresh evergreen cones (pine, spruce, hemlock, birch)
Pimenta diocia	3 oz (90g) allspice berries
Syzygium aromaticum	3 oz (90g) whole cloves
Citrus spp.	1 oz (30g) dried mixed citrus peel slivers (orange, lemon, tangerine, grapefruit, lime, whole dried kumquats, key limes)

TO CREATE THE BOTANICAL BLEND

Cut the tender tips of the fresh evergreens into pieces about 12 in (30cm) long. These can be gathered on a crisp fall day and stored in a cool spot (45°–50°F; 7°–10°C) until you are ready to create your holiday blend.

Cut any large cones into 1-in (2.5-cm) pieces with pruning shears, but keep small cones whole. Store all of them in a paper bag until they are needed.

Select a container that is large enough to hold and roomy enough to mix several quarts of greens and other botanicals.

Cut all the fresh greens, including the branches, into 1-in (2.5-cm) pieces with pruning shears and put them into the container.

Add the cones, allspice berries, cloves, and citrus peel slivers. Mix everything together with your hands. If the evergreen needles are sharp, wear heavy gloves.

Leave the blend in the container for 1 week.

Mix it every day so that the moisture from the fresh greens will be absorbed by the spices and citrus peels. After a few days the fragrances will combine and the blend will develop a personality all its own.

Collect fresh evergreen cones. Store-bought cones have little fragrance, so use them only if you are unable to find fresh ones.

NEW ENGLAND WEDDING HERBS
An Herbal Mix

TIME INVOLVED
Assembly • 30 minutes

ᴸong associated with brides and weddings, this lovely, fragrant mix of herbs and flowers is used lavishly throughout wedding celebrations. Fill a small decorative box with it, attach a pretty card explaining the significance of the herbs, and give it to the newlyweds as a memento of the happy occasion. Or strew handfuls on the tables at the wedding reception, leaving a small card at each place setting listing the bridal couple's names, wedding date, and herbal meanings (see "Language of Flowers," pages 32–33).

You may also want to fill some simple sachets with the mix and give them as wedding favors. Or heap beautiful silver or cut glass bowls with the wedding herbs and pass them to guests after the wedding ceremony so that they can shower the happy couple with herbal blessings.

Tools & Utensils

Small kitchen scale with a weighing basket

Large glass, stainless steel, pottery, or enamel mixing bowl

Stainless steel spoon

Botanicals

Rosa spp.	2½ oz (75g) rose petals and flowers
Origanum majorana	½ oz (15g) marjoram
Lavandula angustifolia	½ oz (15g) lavender
Rosmarinus officinalis	½ oz (15g) rosemary
Myrtus communis	¼ oz (7g) myrtle

To Assemble the Herbal Mix

Place the rose petals and flowers, marjoram, lavender, rosemary, and myrtle in a large mixing bowl.
Stir them together with a stainless steel spoon.

ᵀhe herbs and flowers called for in this recipe are not the only ones traditionally found in wedding mixes. Often included are sage, to symbolize good health, long life, and domestic virtue; ivy leaves, to signify friendship; blue salvia, to express "I think of you"; and fennel seeds, to say "worthy of all praise."

ENGLISH FARMHOUSE
A Botanical Blend

TIME INVOLVED
Assembly • 30 minutes

*D*ISPLAY THIS VERY ENGLISH, VIBRANT-SMELLING botanical blend in an ironstone bowl or an old wooden container. Fill sachets with it and tie them to the backs of chairs or hang them on doorknobs. Each time the bags are brushed or slightly crushed, a clean, fresh scent will perfume the air.

Botanicals

Rosa spp.	3 oz (90g) red rose petals
Lavandula angustifolia	3½ oz (100g) lavender
Aloysia triphylla	2 oz (60g) lemon verbena leaves
Santalum album	1 oz (30g) sandalwood chips
Citrus limon	3 oz (90g) dried lemon peel
Cinnamomum zeylanicum	2 oz (60g) soft cinnamon quills

Tools & Utensils

Small kitchen scale with a weighing basket

Large glass, stainless steel, pottery, or enamel mixing bowl

Stainless steel spoon

TO ASSEMBLE THE BOTANICAL BLEND

Pour the rose petals, lavender, lemon verbena leaves, and sandalwood chips into a large mixing bowl.

Crumple both the lemon peel and cinnamon quills over the mix to release their fragrant oils.

Blend the botanicals together, with a stainless steel spoon. Try to keep the lemon verbena leaves whole.

BLUE HEAVEN

TIME INVOLVED
Making the scent • 30 minutes
Assembly • 1 hour

THE RECIPE FOR THIS BEAUTIFUL BLUE AND PURPLE POTPOURRI comes from one of Australia's many lavender farms. Its complex, sophisticated fragrance is underlined by the familiar scent of lavender. It does not require aging.

Botanicals

Mentha spp.	3 oz (90g) mint (eau de cologne, apple, or spearmint)
Consolida regalis	2½ oz (75g) blue, white, and purple larkspur flowers
Lavandula angustifolia	3 oz (90g) lavender flowers
Cinnamomum cassia	8 cinnamon sticks
Myristica fragrans	1 whole nutmeg

Fixatives

Styrax spp.	1 Tbsp (15g) gum benzoin
Iris germanica var. *florentina*	4 Tbsp (60g) cut and dried orrisroot chunks
	2 Tbsp (30g) Epsom salts

Oils

6 drops violet oil
8 drops lavender oil
6 drops rose geranium oil
4 drops neroli (orange blossom oil)
5 drops lemon oil
5 drops rose oil
5 drops spearmint oil

Tools & Utensils

Small kitchen scale with a weighing basket

Set of stainless steel measuring spoons

1-gallon (3.8-l) glass jar with a tight-fitting lid

Eyedropper

Hammer or kitchen crushing ball

Nutmeg grater

TO CREATE THE SCENT

Crush, with either a hammer or a crushing ball, the gum benzoin.
Pour it, along with the orrisroot chunks and the Epsom salts, into a gallon-sized (3.8-l) jar.
Use an eyedropper to carefully drip the violet, lavender, rose geranium, orange blossom, lemon, rose, and spearmint oils, a drop at a time, over the fixatives.
Cap the jar tightly and gently shake it to coat the fixatives with the oils.

TO ASSEMBLE THE POTPOURRI

Uncap the jar and add the mint and the larkspur and lavender flowers.
Crumble, using either the hammer or crushing ball, the cinnamon sticks and add to the jar. Grate the nutmeg into the mix.
Recap the jar and gently roll it back and forth in your hands to blend the oiled fixatives with the botanicals.

TEXAS CHRISTMAS

TIME INVOLVED

Making the scent	•	15 minutes
Fixing the scent	•	3–4 days
Assembly	•	1 hour
Aging the mix	•	6–8 weeks

$\mathcal{D}$EVELOPED IN HOT, HUMID SOUTHERN TEXAS, this mix features the crisp, vibrant scents of peppermint and pine, which create a cool match for its sprightly red, white, and green colors. Display it at Christmas in decorative containers, tuck some freshly cut greens or sprigs of fresh eucalyptus around the edges, stir the potpourri gently with your fingers, and enjoy the fragrance.

Tools & Utensils

Small kitchen scale with a weighing basket

Set of stainless steel measuring spoons

1-quart (.95-l) glass jar with a tight-fitting lid

Eyedropper

Large glass, stainless steel, pottery, or enamel mixing bowl

Sharp scissors or small garden clippers

Stainless steel spoon

Two 1-gallon (3.8-l) nonplastic containers with tight-fitting lids

Botanicals

Celosia cristata	2 oz (60g) crested red cockscomb
Gomphrena globosa	2 oz (60g) white globe amaranth flowers
Limonium dumosa	2 oz (60g) German statice, cut into 1-in (2.5-cm) pieces
Centaurea rothrockii	2 oz (60g) basket flower seed heads
Helichrysum bracteatum	40 red and white strawflower heads
Rosmarinus officinalis	2 oz (60g) rosemary
Eucalyptus spp.	½ oz (15g) eucalyptus leaves
Laurus nobilis	1 oz (30g) Mediterranean bay leaves
Evernia prunastri	½ oz (15g) oakmoss, snipped into ½-in (1.3-cm) pieces

Fixatives

Tsuga spp.; Juniperus spp.;	2 oz (60g) assorted small evergreen cones
Cedrus spp.; Abies balsamea	(hemlock, juniper, cedar, balsam fir)

Oils

½ tsp (2.5ml) cinnamon oil
¼ tsp (1.3ml) peppermint oil
¼ tsp (1.3ml) pennyroyal oil
¼ tsp (1.3ml) wintergreen oil

To Create the Scent

Put the evergreen cones into a 1-quart (.95-l) glass jar.

Use an eyedropper to drip the cinnamon, peppermint, pennyroyal, and wintergreen oils, a drop at a time, over the cones.

Cap the jar with a tight-fitting lid and shake vigorously to coat the cones with the oils. (Although any small evergreen cones can be used, hemlock absorbs oils especially well.)

To Fix the Scent

Let the oiled cones sit in the sealed jar for 3–4 days. Shake the jar daily without opening it, as exposure to the air will dissipate the volatile oils.

To Assemble the Potpourri

Prepare the crested red cockscomb for weighing by snipping off most of the flat woody stem under the velvety head and discarding it.

Break the flower heads into 1–1½ in (2.5–3.8cm) in size pieces.

Combine the flower head pieces and the globe amaranth flowers, statice, basket flowers, strawflowers, rosemary, eucalyptus and bay leaves, oakmoss, and the scented cones in a large mixing bowl.

Stir well with a stainless steel spoon, folding the cones into the leaves and flowers.

Pack the mix into two separate gallon-size (3.8-l) containers, cap them with tight-fitting lids, and allow them to mature for 6–8 weeks.

CAMBRIA CHRISTMAS

TIME INVOLVED

Making the scent •	5 minutes
Fixing the scent •	3–4 days
Assembly •	45 minutes
Aging the mix •	2–4 weeks

*G*REEN BAY LEAVES, RED ROSE PETALS, POMEGRANATES, and red globe amaranth mingled with the traditional fragrances of rosemary, apple, and cinnamon help bring Christmas to this quaint village on the California coast. Use sprigs of fresh rosemary either to decorate the top of the potpourri or to form a wreath around the base of the display container.

Tools & Utensils

Small kitchen scale with a weighing basket

Set of stainless steel measuring spoons

Small glass jar with a tight-fitting lid

Eyedropper

Stainless steel spoon

1–gallon (3.8-l) glass jar with a tight-fitting lid

Botanicals

Rosa spp.	4 oz (120g) red rose petals
Punica granatum var. *nana*	5–8 miniature pomegranates
Gomphrena globosa	1 oz (30g) red globe amaranth flowers
Cinnamomum cassia	2 oz (60g) large cinnamon chips and pieces
Umbellularia officinalis	1 oz (30g) California bay leaves
Rosmarinus officinalis	2 oz (60g) dried rosemary

Fixatives

Iris germanica var. *florentina*	7 Tbsp (105g) cut and dried orrisroot chunks
Iris germanica var. *florentina*	2 tsp (10g) orrisroot powder

Oils

½ tsp (2.5ml) apple fragrance oil
¼ tsp (1.25ml) cinnamon oil

To Create the Scent

Place the orrisroot chunks and powder in a small glass jar. Using an eyedropper, drip the apple and cinnamon oils, a drop at a time, onto the orrisroot chunks and powder.

Stir the oils and orrisroot chunks and powder together with a stainless steel spoon to blend the mixture thoroughly.

Cap the jar with a tight-fitting lid and set aside for 3–4 days.

To Assemble the Potpourri

Place the oiled orrisroot mixture in a gallon-size (3.8-l) glass jar.

Add the rose petals, pomegranates, globe amaranth flowers, cinnamon, bay leaves, and rosemary to the top of the oiled orrisroot mixture.

Cap the jar with a tight-fitting lid and shake gently to blend. Allow the potpourri to mature for 2–4 weeks.

NEW ZEALAND PINEWOOD

TIME INVOLVED

Assembly • 25 minutes

Aging the mix • 4–6 weeks

*T*HIS SIMPLE POTPOURRI CALLS FOR FOUR WIDELY AVAILABLE INGREDIENTS—all green—plus a few drops of essential oils. It was concocted by Olive Dunn of New Zealand from botanicals in her half-acre garden, which is intensively planted with fragrant herbs and flowers.

Botanicals

Laurus nobilis	½ oz (15g) dried Mediterranean bay leaves
Eucalyptus globulus	½ oz (15g) dried silver-dollar eucalyptus leaves
Rosmarinus officinalis	9 oz (250g) dried rosemary needles
Picea abies	2 oz (60g) dried spruce needles

Oils

10 drops juniper oil

10 drops lime oil

10 drops cedar oil

TO ASSEMBLE THE POTPOURRI

Tear the bay leaves and eucalyptus leaves into small jagged pieces and place them in a gallon-size (3.8-l) glass jar.

Add the rosemary needles and spruce needles to the jar.

Use an eyedropper to drip the juniper, lime, and cedar oils, a drop at a time, onto the botanicals.

Cap the jar with a tight-fitting lid and shake gently to blend the botanicals and oils.

Allow the mix to mature for 4–6 weeks. Shake the jar daily.

Tools & Utensils

Small kitchen scale with a weighing basket

1-gallon (3.8-l) glass jar with a tight-fitting lid

Eyedropper

*T*he heart of this mix is its vibrant, joyous, robust combination of rosemary and lime. The scent is so energizing, so refreshing, and so soul-satisfying that the mix should be heaped in big bowls placed inside the entrance to your home or office or in your kitchen and bathroom.

GREEN HORIZONS CHRISTMAS

TIME INVOLVED

Making the scent • 10 minutes
Assembly • 45 minutes
Aging the mix • 3–4 weeks

HERE ARE SO MANY AROMATIC WOODY BOTANICALS in this potpourri from the mountains of western Pennsylvania that it can be used as a simmering blend. After you have enjoyed Green Horizons warm, spicy aroma for the holidays, remove the cockscomb, save it for another potpourri, and drop a handful of the remaining mix into a small simmering pot of water. This will ensure that the lovely fragrance lingers throughout your house.

Tools & Utensils

Small kitchen scale with a weighing basket

Set of stainless steel measuring spoons

Large glass, stainless steel, pottery, or enamel mixing bowl

Eyedropper

Stainless steel spoon

Sharp scissors

1-gallon (3.8-l) glass jar with a tight-fitting lid

Botanicals

Celosia cristata	1 oz (30g) crested red cockscomb
Rosmarinus officinalis	4 oz (120g) rosemary
Rosa spp.	8 oz (225g) rose hips
Illicium verum	2 oz (60g) star anise
Cinnamomum cassia	8 oz (225g) cinnamon chips
Pimenta dioica	1½ oz (45g) allspice berries
Buxus sempervirens	1 oz (30g) boxwood leaves
Syzygium aromaticum	1 oz (30g) whole cloves
Tsuga spp.; Picea spp.; Betula spp.; Alnus spp.	¼ oz (7g) assorted small evergreen cones (hemlock, spruce, birch, alder)
Juniperus virginiana	¼ oz (7g) dried red cedar tips

Fixatives

Iris germanica var. *florentina*	4 oz (120g) cut and dried orrisroot chunks

Oils

1 tsp (5ml) cinnamon oil
1 tsp (5ml) balsam oil
1 tsp (5ml) pine or fir oil

TO CREATE THE SCENT

Place the orrisroot chunks in a large mixing bowl. Use an eyedropper to drip the cinnamon, balsam, and pine or fir oils, a drop at a time, onto the orrisroot.
Stir the orrisroot chunks and oils together with a stainless steel spoon until the chunks are well coated with the oils.

TO ASSEMBLE THE POTPOURRI

Prepare the crested red cockscomb for weighing by snipping off most of the flat woody stem under the velvety head and discard.
Break the flower heads into pieces 1–1½ in (2.5–3.8cm) in size. Add them and the remaining botanicals to the mixing bowl containing the oiled orrisroot.
Stir thoroughly with the stainless steel spoon. Pack the mix into a gallon-sized (3.8-l) glass jar and cap with a tight-fitting lid.
Allow the potpourri to mature for 3–4 weeks. Shake the jar well each day to ensure that the ingredients are fully blended.

MARYLAND'S COLONIAL ROSE

TIME INVOLVED

Making the scent • 10 minutes
Assembly • 45 minutes
Aging the mix • 3–4 weeks

*T*HIS DELICATE FLORAL BLEND is the result of an inspired marriage of two early American recipes. Its colonial Maryland heritage fits well with rooms adorned with richly colored oriental rugs, highly polished mahogany furniture, and glowing brass accessories.

Botanicals

Rosa spp.	4 oz (120g) rose petals
	4 oz (120g) mixed flower petals
Rosa spp.	1 oz (30g) Moroccan rosebuds
Lavandula angustifolia	2 oz (60g) lavender
Pogostemon cablin	2 oz (60g) patchouli leaves
Coriandrum sativum	½ oz (15g) coriander seeds, crushed
Boswellia carteri	½ oz (15g) frankincense tears, crushed
Dipteryx odorata	2 tonka beans, roughly chopped
Cinnamomum cassia	5 broken 4-in (10-cm) cinnamon sticks,
Citrus spp.	2 oz (60g) thread-cut dried citrus peels (lemon, orange, lime, tangerine, or grapefruit)
Elettaria cardamomum	¼ oz (7g) cardamom seeds, crushed
Santalum freycetiarum	2 oz (60g) sandalwood chips
Pimenta dioica	½ oz (15g) whole allspice berries

Fixatives

Iris germanica var. *florentina*	1 oz (30g) orrisroot powder

Oils

12 drops rose oil
5 drops patchouli oil

Tools & Utensils

Small kitchen scale with a weighing basket

Small glass, stainless steel, pottery, or enamel mixing bowl

Eyedropper

Stainless steel spoon

Large glass, stainless steel, pottery, or enamel mixing bowl

1-gallon (3.8-l) glass jar with a tight-fitting lid

To Create the Scent

Place the orrisroot powder in a small mixing bowl. Using an eyedropper, drip the rose and patchouli oils, a drop at a time, onto the orrisroot and stir with a stainless steel spoon until the powder completely absorbs the oils.

To Assemble the Potpourri

Place all of the botanicals in a large mixing bowl and stir gently with the stainless steel spoon.

Sprinkle the oiled orrisroot powder over the botanicals and stir the mix again carefully but thoroughly with the stainless steel spoon.

Pack the potpourri into a gallon-sized (3.8-l) glass jar and cap with a tight-fitting lid. Let the mix mature for 3–4 weeks. Rock the jar gently once a day to keep the oiled orrisroot powder distributed throughout the mix.

LUSCIOUS LEMON

TIME INVOLVED
Making the scent • 10 minutes
Assembly • 40 minutes

HEN THE HOT, MUGGY AIR OF SUMMER hangs over the heartland cornfields, the cool, soft, sage green shades of this potpourri are as soothing to the eye as its lemony aroma is refreshing to the soul. This Indiana-born mixture can be used immediately after mixing; no aging is required.

Botanicals

Myrica cerifera	3 oz (90g) tallow berries
Illicium verum	2 oz (60g) star anise
Betula spp.; Tsuga spp.; Alnus spp.; Pinus spp.	¼ oz (7g) assorted small evergreen cones (birch, hemlock, alder, pine)
Aloysia triphylla	4 oz (120g) whole lemon verbena leaves
Citrus limon	1½ oz (45g) lemon peel, cut into 1-in (2.5-cm) pieces
Cymbopogon citratus	½ oz (15g) lemongrass, cut into 1-in (2.5-cm) pieces
Nigella damascena	½ oz (15g) nigella seedpods
Citrus limon	6 whole lemon slices
Hydrangea macrophylla	¼ oz (7g) hydrangea flower clusters

Fixatives

Evernia prunastri	4 Tbsp (60g) oakmoss, cut into ½-in (1.3-cm) pieces

Oils
¼ tsp (1.3ml) lemon oil
¼ tsp (1.3ml) lemon verbena oil

Tools & Utensils

Small kitchen scale with a weighing basket

Set of stainless steel measuring spoons

Sharp scissors

Large glass, stainless steel, pottery, or enamel mixing bowl

Eyedropper

Stainless steel spoon

TO CREATE THE SCENT

Place the cut oakmoss in the bottom of a large mixing bowl.
Use an eyedropper to drip the lemon and lemon verbena oils, a drop at a time, over the oakmoss.
Stir the mix gently with a stainless steel spoon until the oakmoss is well coated with the oils.

TO ASSEMBLE THE POTPOURRI

Snip the clusters of tallow berries from their heavy stems.
Put the berries, star anise, and small evergreen cones in the mixing bowl containing the oiled oakmoss so that they can absorb some of the oils.
Add the lemon verbena leaves, lemon peel, lemongrass, and nigella seedpods to the mixing bowl and stir gently but thoroughly with the stainless steel spoon. Try to keep the leaves and pods whole.
Pour the mix into a pretty container and decorate the top of the potpourri with the lemon slices and hydrangea flower clusters.

MINNESOTA HARVEST MOON

TIME INVOLVED

Making the scent	•	5 minutes
Fixing the scent	•	20 minutes
Assembly	•	45 minutes
Aging the mix	•	4–6 weeks

*T*HE SOFT, SWEET SCENT OF CHERRY VANILLA dominates this rich, romantic potpourri.

Botanicals

Rosa spp.	2 oz (60g) rose petals
Ocimum basilicum purpureum	1 oz (30g) dark opal basil
Mentha spicata or *Mentha piperata*	½ oz (15g) mint
Ocimum basilicum	½ oz (15g) green basil

Fixatives

Iris germanica var. *florentina*	4 Tbsp (60g) cut and dried orrisroot chunks

Oils

1 tsp (5ml) cherry oil
1 tsp (5ml) vanilla oil
1 tsp (5ml) heliotrope oil

TO CREATE THE SCENT

Place the orrisroot chunks in a small glass jar.
Use an eyedropper to drip the cherry, vanilla, and heliotrope oils, a drop at a time, onto the orrisroot.
Cap the jar with a tight-fitting lid and shake well to blend.

TO FIX THE SCENT

Allow the oiled orrisroot chunks to sit for 20 minutes.

TO ASSEMBLE THE POTPOURRI

Place the rose petals, dark opal basil, mint, and green basil in a gallon-size (3.8-l) glass jar.
Add the oiled orrisroot, cover the jar with a tight-fitting lid, and gently shake until the orrisroot is mixed thoroughly with the botanicals.
Allow the potpourri to mature for 4–6 weeks. Shake the jar once a week to ensure that the orrisroot mixes well with the petals and leaves, but don't remove the lid.

Tools & Utensils

Small kitchen scale with a weighing basket

Set of stainless steel measuring spoons

Small glass jar with a tight-fitting lid

Eyedropper

1-gallon (3.8-l) glass jar with a tight-fitting lid

WOODLAND WALK

TIME INVOLVED

Making the scent	•	30 minutes
Fixing the scent	•	7 days
Assembly	•	1 hour
Aging the mix	•	4 weeks

A FRAGRANT STILL LIFE, PEACEFUL AND REFRESHING both to view and to smell, this potpourri is reminiscent of the lush fields and woods of the Hudson River valley of New York State.

As you gather woodland materials for this potpourri, take the time to pick up fallen leaves to use in decorating. Choose ones that feel tough and leathery, such as those from oaks, Bradford pears, and magnolias. They have a natural waxlike coating that serves to preserve a small amount of moisture in them. As a result, these leaves can be used for indoor decorating for several weeks before they become so crisp that they crumble. Gather the leaves singly or in attractively shaped sprays. Press them lightly under a rug or between newspapers weighted down by a heavy book for 3–4 days to prevent excessive curling. Use them as decorative accents on mirrors and tabletops, or add them to autumn arrangements composed of fruits, vegetables, nuts, and berries.

Tools & Utensils

Small kitchen scale with a weighing basket

Set of stainless steel measuring spoons

1-quart (.95-l) glass jar with a tight-fitting lid

Eyedropper

Two 1-gallon (3.8-l) glass jars with tight-fitting lids

Sharp scissors

Botanicals

Pinus spp., Querus robur, Betula pendula	2 oz (60g) mixture of woodland materials, such as small pinecones, dried seedpods, acorns and nuts, dried fungus, dried lichens, and torn birch bark
Hypnum currifolium	1 oz (30g) dried sheet moss
	3 oz (90g) brightly colored autumn leaves
Oaultheria	1 oz (30g) lemon leaf

Fixatives

Iris germanica var. *florentina*	1½ oz (45g) cut and dried orrisroot chunks
Evernia prunastri	3 Tbsp (50g) oakmoss, cut into ½-in (1.3-cm) pieces

Oils

3 Tbsp (45ml) Woodland Walk fragrance oil

To Create the Scent

Put the orrisroot chunks and cut-up oakmoss into a 1-quart (.95-l) glass jar. Using an eyedropper, drip 1 Tbsp (15ml) Woodland Walk fragrance oil, a drop at a time, over them.

Cap the jar with a tight-fitting lid and shake vigorously. Allow the mixture to mature for 7 days.

Put the woodland materials and sheet moss into a gallon-size (3.8-l) glass jar. Using an eyedropper, drip the remaining 2 Tbsps (30ml) of fragrance oil, a drop at a time, over them.

Cap the jar with a tight-fitting lid and allow the mixture to mature for 7 days. Shake the jar well each day.

To Assemble the Potpourri

Scatter some of the oiled orrisroot chunks and oakmoss on the bottom of a second gallon-size (3.8-l) jar.

Add a layer of the woodland materials. Then add the autumn and lemon leaves. Continue alternating layers until you have used up all the botanicals.

Cap the jar tightly and let it sit for 24 hours. Every day for the next 4 weeks, gently "rock your crock,"—that is, roll the jar gently in your hands. At the end of that time, the oils should have fully impregnated all the materials.

Pour the potpourri into a wooden bowl, an old crock, or a rustic twig basket. Arrange some leaves and unusual pods or nuts on the top of the potpourri to create a woodland still life.

If you have gathered potpourri ingredients, such as cones, pods, leaves, mosses, and nuts, during woodland walks, it is wise to treat them with either heat or cold to destroy any animal or insect life they may harbor.

Lemon leaf, or salal, is a large, leathery green leaf used extensively by florists, who should easily be able to supply your needs. You can dry the leaves either by standing the stems upright in a jar or by hanging them upside down in a dimly lit, warm, moisture-free place.

The Craft Room

Creating handmade gifts and decorative home accessories is a relaxing and rewarding way to spend your free time. All of the projects included here were chosen with the busy, time-pinched crafter in mind. Each project can be made within one or two hours.

Many, such as the Shoe Stuffers and Simple Sachets (pages 94–95), Scented Beads and Ornaments (pages 84–87), and the Herbal Bath Scrub (pages 124–25), are wonderful projects to teach groups of older children or to use as fundraisers for clubs and fairs. Others, like the seasonal Halloween Herb Door Bunch (pages 96–99) and the Cambria Christmas Garlands (pages 108–111), add lovely accents to the home. The Orange Peel Heart Wreath (pages 82–83) represents recycling at its best, while the Quick and Simple Wedding Herb Favors (pages 104–5) can add a charming and loving touch to a wedding reception.

SIMPLE FLORIST'S BOW

A SIMPLE FLORIST'S BOW IS MADE BY LOOPING a length of ribbon into a figure 8. A piece of fine-gauge florist's wire is bound around the center point of the ribbon to secure the bow. It has two loops of equal size and two tails of equal length. A complex bow, on the other hand, is made by building up several layers of figure-8 ribbon loops, one on top of another. A piece of florist's wire is twisted around the center of these ribbons in a similar fashion to create the bow.

STEP-BY-STEP

1 Place the free end of a length of ribbon flat in the palm of your hand. Let a portion of the ribbon hang over the edge of your hand. With your thumb and forefinger, pinch the ribbon at the point where it begins to hang. This is now the center of the bow.

2 Form the first loop (or half of the figure 8) by expanding the long piece of ribbon upward, then loop it back to the center of the bow. Slide the ribbon between your thumb and forefinger to hold the first loop in place.

3 Make a second loop, the same size as the first loop, by bringing the loose end of the ribbon up toward you and then loop it back to the center of the bow. Slide the end between your thumb and forefinger. You should have two loops and two streamers of equal size. Cut the ribbon from the spool.

4 Loop a piece of 28-gauge florist's wire around the center of the bow. Then pull the two ends of the wire to the back of the bow and twist them together tightly.

Florist's bows can be made with either single- or double-faced ribbon. The weave of a double-faced ribbon appears the same on both sides, whereas a single-faced ribbon has front and back sides. The front, or right, side is usually shiny or displays a pattern; the wrong side is dull and bears no pattern. If you use single-sided ribbon to make a florist's bow, be sure to start with the ribbon right side up in the palm of your hand.

ORANGE PEEL HEART WREATH

ON'T RESTRICT YOURSELF TO ORANGES FOR THIS PROJECT. Lemon, grapefruit, tangerine, and lime peels also make interesting fragrant wreaths. Use them singly or in patterned combinations.

If you plan to give a citrus peel wreath as a gift, place it in a box on a bed of citrus potpourri, such as Luscious Lemon (page 74), Silver Bay Citrus (page 50), or even New Zealand Pinewood (page 71), with its marvelous lime and rosemary fragrance.

TIME INVOLVED

Assembly • 1½ hours

Drying time • 3–4 hours in a dehydrator; 4 days to air-dry

Tools & Materials

Peels from 5 or 6 large oranges

Sharp knife

Cutting board

14 in (35cm) 20- or 22-gauge florist's wire or lightweight coathanger wire

Flat basket or screen dehydrator

12 in (30-cm) raffia

4 lengths of ⅛-in-wide (3-mm) 12-in-long (30-cm) satin ribbon

2 or 3 tiny pinecones or dried rosehips

6 in (15cm) 28-gauge or fine florist's wire

White glue or Quick-drying glue

1 Save the fresh peels from five or six juiced oranges. Pull the membranes away from the peels.

2 Cut each peel into strips ½–¾ in (1.3–2cm) wide, then cut each of these into equal-sized squares. Don't worry if your pieces aren't perfectly square; the odd shapes will blend in nicely.

3 Make a 1-in (2.5-cm) right-angled hook at one end of the florist's wire to prevent the citrus squares from sliding off while you string them. Thread the other end of the wire through the center of a peel square, pushing the square down the wire to the end that has the right-angled hook. String the remaining peel squares.

4 Twist the two ends of the wire together, and shape the wreath into a plump heart. The wire joint becomes the top, center of the heart. Lay the heart wreath in a flat basket or dehydrator in a very warm spot (80°–95°F; 27°–35°C) and let it dry for 4–6 days. Turn the wreath each day to prevent the peels from developing mold.

5 When the heart is dry, tie two 12-in (30-cm) lengths of ribbon onto the wreath. Dry citris peels are firm to the touch.

6 Treat the raffia and two lengths of satin ribbon as one piece and form them into a figure-8 bow (page 81). With your thumb and forefinger, pinch the bow in the center and hold it in place by twisting the two ends of the wire that hold the wreath together around the center of the bow. Lay the wreath flat and, with quick-drying glue, stick on the pinecones or dried rosehips for decorations.

As they dry, the peel squares shrink; gaps can develop if you don't string citrus peels close together. In order to have a full-looking finished wreath, compress and add as many squares as possible.

SCENTED BEADS AND ORNAMENTS

TIME INVOLVED

1½–2 hours

Tools & Materials

Set of stainless steel
measuring spoons

Electric coffee or
spice grinder

Small glass, stainless steel,
pottery, or enamel
mixing bowl

Eyedropper

Stainless steel spoon

Petroleum jelly

1 spool of 24- or 26-gauge
florist's wire

Scissors

Shoe box

CENTED BEADS CAN be made into unusual necklaces of varying lengths, or used as fragrant accents on Thanksgiving and Christmas decorations.

In the autumn, string eye-catching patterns of hemlock cones, spice beads, and whole spices, such as allspice berries, juniper berries, and star anise pieces, into long, chunky necklaces to wear over heavy sweaters and woolen shirts. You can also use the same materials, plus slightly larger pinecones, dried lime or lemon slices, chunks of citrus peel, dried rosehips, whole bay leaves, and small whole dried pomegranates, to make garlands for decorating mantels, stairways, and tables during the winter holidays. Drape tabletop-size evergreen trees with ropes of ¾-in (19-mm) rose and spice beads, scented pinecones, small whole dried pomegranates, dried orange slices, dried cranberries, and whole dried pink roses or standard-size red carnations.

Rose-Scented Beads
Makes 60–70 beads

3 Tbsp (50g) finely powdered potpourri, such as Lavender House Rose Garden (page 42) or other fragrant plant material

2 Tbsp (30g) white bread flour

1 mounded Tbsp (15g) powder orrisroot

15 drops essential oil (Choose a fragrance, such as Rose or Rose Geranium that will accentuate the scent of the potpourri or powdered plant material.)

3½–4 Tbsp (47.5–60ml) water

1 Before you begin, place 3 Tbsp (50g) of potpourri in an electric coffee or spice grinder. Grind and regrind until the potpourri has been reduced to a fine powder. Measure 3 Tbsp (50g) of the powdered potpourri into a small mixing bowl. Add the flour and orrisroot powder and blend well.

2 Using an eyedropper, carefully drip the essential oil, a drop at a time, over the top of the dry ingredients.

3 Sprinkle 1 Tbsp (15ml) of water over the ingredients and stir well with a stainless steel spoon. Add the remaining water, 1 Tbsp (15ml) at a time, and continue to stir the ingredients until a pliable paste forms. If necessary, add extra drops of water or an extra sprinkle of orrisroot powder to achieve a workable consistency.

4 Coat your hands lightly with petroleum jelly. Knead the scented paste for about 1 minute. This action develops a substance in the flour called gluten, whose elastic qualities help prevent the paste from cracking as it dries.

5 Pinch off small pieces of paste and roll into beads about ⅜ in (10mm) in diameter, until you have used up the mix.

6 Thread the beads onto wires that are long enough to span the length of a shoe box. Leave a small space empty at each end of the wires.

7 Punch holes opposite each other in the sides of the shoe box. Push the ends of the filled wire into the holes from the inside, turning the "tails" at each end up over the rim of the shoe box and twisting them back onto the wire inside the container. You should now have "clotheslines" of mauve-colored, rose-scented beads stretched securely across the drying container. Hanging the beads over a container allows free air circulation, so that the beads dry uniformly and quickly. Place the container in a dark, warm spot, and rotate the beads each day. They will take 4–7 days to dry, depending on air temperature and humidity levels.

Store the dried beads in a glass jar with a tight-fitting lid, away from high humidity, until you are ready to use them.

VARIATIONS

Experiment with different-shaped beads; roll the paste into tubes, ovals, cubes, and rectangles. You can even roll the scented dough out between two sheets of waxed paper as you would a piecrust. With tiny, canape-sized cookie cutters, cut out hearts, stars, and other interesting shapes. Using a toothpick or short piece of thin wire, make a hole at the top of each shape, then place the cutouts on wax paper to dry. Treat them like beads or slip narrow satin ribbon through the holes and hang them as miniature ornaments.

Scented beads can be made from individual plants as well as from potpourris and spice blends. Try forming beads from powdered dried rose petals, sage leaves, lemon balm leaves, mint leaves, and scented geranium leaves, or from ground spices, such as cinnamon, cloves, ginger, allspice, or nutmeg. Keep in mind that all the plant material must be fully dried and finely powdered.

CAR FRAGRANCE BAG

TIME INVOLVED

1 hour

Tools & Materials

1 piece of fabric, 12 x 18 in
(30 x 45cm)

Sewing scissors

Sewing machine or needle
and thread

2–5 oz (60–150g) potpourri

2 Velcro strips, 4½ in
(11cm) long, with
self-adhesive backing

HINT OF FRAGRANCE IN YOUR CAR CAN PROVE REFRESHING, particularly if you are faced with a long commute. When selecting a potpourri, look to the lemony citrus scents and the piney woods mixes for stimulation and revival and to the floral and rose blends for a peaceful, calming effect.

STEP-BY-STEP

1 Fold the piece of fabric in half, wrong side out. Sew around two sides of the fabric, leaving one side open.

2 Fold the raw edges of the opening ½ in (13mm) along the bag. Press with an iron to make a sharp crease.

3 Turn the bag right side out and fill with potpourri.

4 Hand-sew the opening closed with a whip stitch.

5 Peel the protective backing from the Velcro strips and stick them onto the back of the fragrance bag.

Peel the protective covering from the tops of the Velcro strips and attach the bag to the back of the front seat, interior wall, or ceiling of your car.

FRAGRANT WRITING PAPER

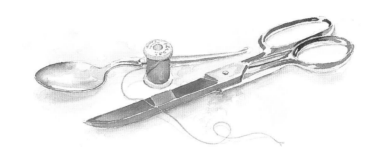

T͟O LIGHTLY SCENT WRITING PAPER AND NOTE CARDS, add some potpourri, such as Lavender House Rose Garden (page 42), to a gossamer bag of tulle, then tuck it into a box of stationery.

TIME INVOLVED
45 minutes

Tools & Materials

Sewing scissors

Pinking shears

1¼ ft (1m) 6-in-wide (15-cm) tulle

Needle

Thread to match tulle color

½ oz (15g) potpourri (about 7 Tbsp)

Stainless steel spoon

STEP-BY-STEP

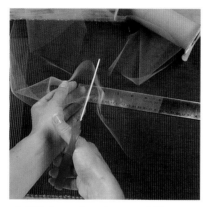

1 With the sewing scissors or pinking shears, cut the tulle into two pieces, each 5 x 7 in (12 x 18cm).

2 Using a running stitch, sew around three sides of the tulle; leave one side open.

3 Fill the bag with potpourri. Stitch the fourth side of the bag closed.

4 Trim around all four sides of the bag with the pinking shears.

GARDENIA BATH OIL

*I*T IS EASY TO TURN A DAILY BATH INTO A SENSUOUS, LUXURIOUS EXPERIENCE. Just add a tablespoon (15ml) of fragrant bath oil to a tub of warm bath water. The scent will help you relax while the oil smoothes and nourishes your skin. Even the most elegant-looking bath oil takes only minutes to create.

TIME INVOLVED
30 minutes

Tools & Materials

Sharp scissors

Sprig of white larkspur

Sprig of California bay leaves, about the same length as the larkspur, or 3 or 4 long bay leaves

3 or 4 white globe amaranth flower heads

3 or 4 dried gardenia petals

1 or 2 perfect white rose petals

4 or 5 uva-ursi leaves

Decorative clear glass bottle with stopper or cap

Sweet almond or apricot oil to fill the bottle

Glass, stainless steel, pottery, or enamel mixing bowl

Eyedropper

20 drops bay essential oil

Stainless steel spoon

Funnel

Piece of ribbon or raffia

STEP-BY-STEP

1 Cut the stems of the larkspur and bay leaves so that they are slightly shorter than the height of the bottle. Place the sprigs of larkspur and bay leaves, globe amaranths, gardenia and rose petals, and uva-ursi leaves in a decorative clear glass bottle.

2 Pour the almond or apricot oil into a mixing bowl. Then, using an eyedropper, drip the bay essential oil, a drop at a time, into the almond or apricot oil.

3 Stir the two oils together with a stainless steel spoon. Then, using a funnel, pour the combined oils into the clear glass bottle.

4 Cap the bottle and tie a beautiful ribbon or piece of raffia around the neck of the bottle. If you plan to give the bath oil as a gift, add a decorative tag with instructions for use. Allow the mix to mature for at least a week before using.

The following potpourri recipes also make fragrant bath oils:

Silver Bay Citrus (page 50)

Use 3 or 4 pieces of slivered orange peel, 1 or 2 sticks of cinnamon, 2 or 3 whole cloves, and a whole vanilla bean. Add 10 drops each of essential oil of lemon and orange, as well as 3 drops of vanilla oil.

Luscious Lemon (page 74)

Use 3 or 4 lemon verbena leaves, 2 or 3 strips of lemon peel, 3 or 4 small cones, 3 or 4 nigella pods, and a few pieces of star anise. Add 10 drops each of lemon oil and lemon verbena oil.

Catalpa Plantation Herb Garden (page 43)

Use 3 or 4 whole roses or rosebuds, 2 or 3 rose petals, 3 or 4 whole lemon verbena leaves, 1 or 2 long stems of lavender, and 2 or 3 whole chamomile flowers. Add 20 drops of lavender oil.

CAUTION!

When modifying potpourri recipes for use in bath oils, follow these guidelines:

- Never use made-up potpourri. Fixative material, such as orrisroot, can cause an allergic reaction.
- Always scent the bath oil with small amounts of essential oils, not fragrance oils. The former are extracted directly from plant material, but the latter are chemically created in a laboratory and, consequently, can sometimes cause an allergic reaction.
- Make sure that all plant material is totally dry before placing it inside the bottle of oil.
- When choosing botanicals, think about how they will look floating in oil. They should be fairly large and pretty to look at. Also, although tiny pieces can be visually attractive, they have a greater chance of escaping from the bottle when the fragrance oil is poured into the bath. Herbs and flowers that are sucked down the drain of a tub can sometimes cause major plumbing problems.

SHOE STUFFERS AND SIMPLE SACHETS

$\mathcal{T}$HESE RICH, AROMATIC BAGS OF HERBS AND SPICES have many household uses. Tuck a few containing strongly fragrant potpourri, such as Aroha Cottage Citrus Zest (page 45), into boots and shoes to keep them fresh smelling. Use a floral fabric with floral potpourri and place the sachets in bureau drawers and on linen shelves to add soft scents, or hang them in closets, where they will impart a subtle lingering fragrance to clothing. Hints of fragrance provide unexpected, welcome flashes of pleasure.

TIME INVOLVED

1½ hours

Tools & Materials

1 piece of lightweight cotton fabric,
6¾ x 9¾ in (17 x 24cm)

Needle and thread or sewing machine

Scissors

Ironing board and iron

½–¾ oz (15–21g) strongly refreshing potpourri

22 in (55cm) ¼-in-wide (6-mm) satin ribbon

Ribbon rose (optional)

STEP-BY-STEP

1 Fold the cotton fabric in half lengthwise, wrong side out, so that it measures about 9¾ x 3¼ in (24 x 8cm). Stitch across the bottom and down the open long side of the fabric.

2 Fold the bag over at the top until the top edge of the fabric is about halfway down the bag. Press well, then turn the bag right side out.

3 Fill the bag about two-thirds full with your chosen potpourri.

4 Tie a ribbon into a bow around the bag, just above the potpourri. Sew a ribbon rosebud in the center if you wish.

HALLOWEEN HERB DOOR BUNCH

TIME INVOLVED

1 hour

Tools & Materials

1 twig swag (nest-sash),
22–24 in (55–60cm) long

1 spool of 26-gauge green
florist's wire

3 lengths of 18-in (45-cm)
24-gauge florist's wire

1 roll ½-in (13-mm)
brown florist's tape

50 in (125cm) raffia

50 in (125cm) narrow red
ribbon or yarn

Florist's scissors

*S*OME HERBS HAVE ALWAYS BEEN ASSOCIATED WITH MAGIC. On Halloween, the spookiest day of the year, protect your home with a generous bundle of hand-tied herbal plant material that has a long been associated with warding off evil spirits.

Oak was the sacred tree of the ancient Celts, who believed that October 31 was a holy day that floated between the end of the old year and the beginning of the new. Yarrow could be used for both good and evil spells as well as fortune telling.

Sage, fennel, and dill were great protecting herbs. Mugwort was too, but only if tied around the waist for a year! Luneria, or silver dollars, was dedicated to the moon, planet of women and witches. Its silvery seedpods were symbolic of pure silver, which offered great protection from evil. Rue was used for blessings and to bestow second sight, but the most protective plant of all was garlic. One clove of the humble garlic was thought to be powerful enough to fend off the greatest evil. Red ribbon or yarn was believed to have the power to combine and intensify the protective qualities of the plants it bound.

Botanicals

2 sprays of 22-in-long (55-cm) dry brown or fresh green oak leaves

3 stems of 22-in (55-cm) golden yarrow

2 stems of 22-in (55-cm) dried mugwort

2 stems of 22-in (55-cm) dried sage

2 stems of 22-in (55-cm) silver dollars

2 stems of 22-in (55-cm) dried fennel heads

8 stems of 14-in (35-cm) rue pods

2 stems of 14-in (35-cm) golden yarrow

1 stem of 14-in (35-cm) dried sage

1 stem of 14-in (35-cm) silver dollars

2 stems of 14-in (35-cm) dill heads

3 whole garlic heads

1 Lay the twig swag on a work surface. Make sure the handle points toward you and the twiggy spray points away from you. Wrap the free end of the spool of 26-gauge wire around the middle of the handle and twist it tightly back onto itself to secure the wire to the form.

2 Arrange one spray of oak leaves on top of the twig form so that the tips of the leaves are about 1 in (2.5cm) shy of the ends of the twigs. Hold the tops of the stems against the handle of the twig form and bind the florist's wire around the stems and handle twice. Pull the wire firmly at each turn. Lay the stems of a second spray of oak leaves beside the first spray and bind it into place. A layer of oak leaves now completely covers the twig form.

3 Place the three stems of 22-in (55-cm) golden yarrow on top of the oak sprays. Position the stems so that the yarrow heads are resting on the top half of the lowest leaves, allowing 2 in (5cm) of the leaves to remain visible. Bind them to the handle, then tie a stem of mugwort on each side of the yarrow.

4 Lay a stem of 22-in (55-cm) sage on top of each piece of mugwort and bind them to the handle. Lay one stem of 22-in (55-cm) silver dollars on each side of the bunch and bind them to the handle. Lay both stems of fennel heads down the center of the bunch and bind them.

5 Bunch the eight stems of rue seedpods together, lay them in the center of the plant material, and bind them to the handle. Place one of the stems of 14-in (35-cm) yarrow on each side of the rue seedpods, and bind them.

6 Position the stem of 14-in (35-cm) sage to the right of one yarrow stem and put the stem of 14-in (35-cm) silver dollars to the left of the other yarrow stem. Bind both stems to the handle. Place both dill heads in the center of the bunch and bind them.

7 Run a length of 24-gauge florist's wire through the top of each garlic head so that there are equal lengths of wire on each side of the garlic heads. Pull the tails of each wire together up over garlic heads and twist them tightly. Cover the wires with florist's tape, stretching and overlapping as you go along to make a smooth, continuous surface.

8 Hold the taped, wired garlics together in your hand and form a flat-backed bunch by pulling one head slightly higher than the other two. Lay the garlic bunch in the center of the cluster of plant material and bind it to the handle. Cut off the binding wire and tie to the form.

9 Tie the raffia and red ribbon into a bow around the handle to hide the wire. Make the loops on the bows about 4 in (10cm) long, with four long tails cascading down the front of the bunch.

MUSLIN MOTH BAGS

TIME INVOLVED

1 hour

Tools & Materials

1 piece of plain muslin, 32 x 38 in (80 x 95cm), washed

Sewing machine

Iron

4–6 oz (120–180g) Cascade Robe Guard (page 47)

Needle and thread

Sharp sewing scissors

*T*HESE LARGE, FLOPPY, UTILITARIAN MOTH BAGS are simple to make. Used generously, they can be very effective in protecting stored woolen clothing from marauding, munching moths. Refill the bags each year to maintain their strong fragrance, and clean clothing before storage.

For added protection, lightly brush the backs of strips of pretty wallpaper with essential oil of cedar. Lay the strips, oiled side down, in storage drawers. Be sure that the oil is dry before placing clean woolens and muslin moth bags in the drawers.

STEP-BY-STEP

1 Fold the piece of muslin in half, wrong side out, and machine-stitch two sides. Leave one side open.

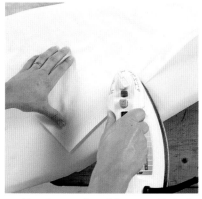

2 Turn the top edge of the open side back about ½ in (13mm) and press firmly into place to form a neat hem.

3 Turn the bag right side out and fill with the herbal mix.

4 Hand-stitch the opening closed and pat the bag flat.

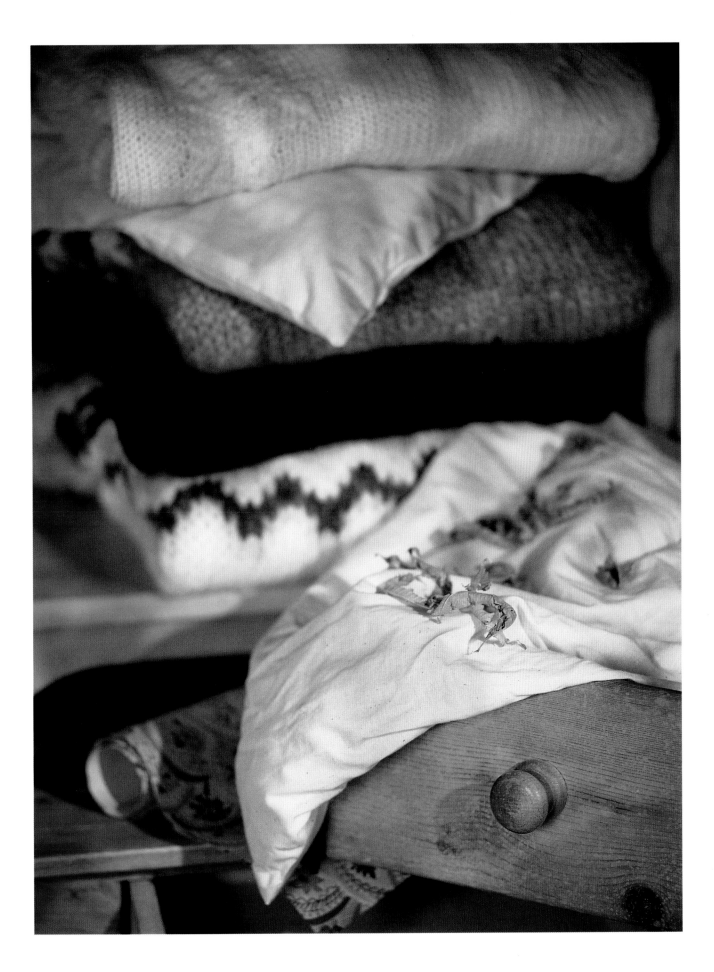

LAVENDER HEARTS

ELICATE, FRAGRANT LAVENDER HEARTS make a charming accent. Hang several hearts in a group over a little girl's bed or around a favorite picture. Lavender Hearts make a nice Mother's Day activity for older children.

TIME INVOLVED
Assembly • 30 minutes
Drying time • 30–60 minutes

Tools & Materials
For a 3-in (7.6-cm) heart

Piece of thin cardboard or sheet of newspaper, about 12 in (30cm) square

White glue

Small dish

9 in (23cm) 20- or 22-gauge florist's wire

1 roll ½-in (13-mm) green or brown florist's tape

½ cup lavender flowers

Small paintbrush

2 lengths of ⅛-in-wide (3-mm), 8-in-long (20-cm) satin ribbon

Quick-drying glue

Rosebud

3 or 4 uva-ursi or boxwood leaves

Sharp scissors

1 Place a piece of cardboard over the work surface. Pour some white glue into a small dish. Bind the florist's wire with the florist's tape, pulling and stretching the tape so that it covers the wire smoothly.

2 Shape the taped wire into a heart and tightly twist the two ends of the wire together. Cover any sharp ends where they join with another piece of florist's tape.

3 Make a 4–5-in (10–12-cm) square bed of lavender on the cardboard. Then, with a paintbrush, coat the wire heart thickly with the glue.

4 Place the heart onto the lavender bed. Using your fingers, cover the heart with the lavender flowers. Allow it to dry in the lavender bed.

Shake off any excess flowers and check the heart for bare spots. If there are any, dab some glue onto them and fill in the area with more lavender flowers. Dry once again.

5 Tie one piece of ribbon around the center point of the top of the heart to form a loop for hanging.

6 Tie the other piece of ribbon into a simple bow with two loops and two tails. Attach the bow with a few dabs of glue.

7 Place a drop of quick-drying glue on the base of the rosebud and tuck it into the center of the bow.

8 Glue the uva-ursi or boxwood leaves, one leaf at a time, around the rosebud, hiding their stem ends under the rosebud to give the appearance of a green halo surrounding the flower.

QUICK AND SIMPLE WEDDING HERB FAVORS

TIME INVOLVED
20 minutes each

Tools & Materials

Piece of cardboard

Felt-tip marker

Sharp scissors

Set of stainless steel
measuring spoons

Ruler

Tulle Sachet
For one sachet

Circle of tulle, 8 in (20cm)
in diameter

1 heaping Tbsp (15g) New
England Wedding Herbs
(page 65)

10 in (25cm)length of
½-inch-wide
(13-mm) twine

Eyelet Wedding Favor
For one favor

8½-in (22-cm) square of
eyelet or other
lightweight fabric

1 tulle sachet

16 in (40cm) ½-in-wide
(13-mm) ribbon

Lace Ribbon Favor
For one favor

10 in (25cm) 2½-in-wide
(6-cm) lace ribbon

Needle and thread in color
to match lace ribbon

1 tulle sachet

14 in (35cm) ¼-in-wide
(6-mm) ribbon

HESE WEDDING, SHOWER, AND ANNIVERSARY FAVORS are easy to make and can be prepared long before they are needed.

First, assemble the New England Wedding Herbs mix in advance and store it in a plastic bag or other closed container. Since there are no oils or fixatives in this blend, you do not need to transfer it to an airtight glass jar. However, if you live in a hot and humid area, it is best to keep the blend in an insect-free environment, such as a refrigerator or freezer.

You can also select the ribbons and fabric early. Cut and carefully store them until you are ready to assemble the favors.

If you want to personalize the favors, allow enough time to inscribe small cards with the names of the bridal couple and their wedding date. Punch holes in each card and attach to the favors with either wired ribbon or fine gold thread.

STEP-BY-STEP Tulle sachet

1 Using an 8-in (20-cm) round plate as a guide, draw a circle on cardboard, then cut out the circle. This will become the template for cutting the tulle.

2 For multiples, fold the tulle as many times as possible, leaving it larger than the plate. Place the template on top of the tulle and cut around the template.

3 Place the New England Wedding Herbs mix in the center of the cut tulle. Gather the ends of the tulle just above the top of the potpourri and tie with the twine.

STEP-BY-STEP Eyelet Wedding Favor

There are 16 Tbsp (240g) per 1-cup measure. To estimate the amount of New England Wedding Herbs you will need, multiply the number of favors by the number of tablespoons (grams) each one requires and divide by 16.

1 With scissors, cut an 8½-in (22-cm) square of eyelet or other lightweight fabric to match the bridal colors.

2 Spread the square on a table. Place the tulle sachet in the center. Gather the ends of the eyelet fabric around the neck of the tulle sachet and tie a bow with the ribbon.

STEP-BY-STEP Lace Ribbon Favor

1 Fold the lace ribbon in half to form a 2½ x 5-in (6 x 12-cm) rectangle.

2 Using the folded edge as the bottom of the sack, sew up the two sides.

3 Place the tulle sachet into the sack. Tie the ribbon into a bow around the lace sack, at the neck of the tulle sachet.

FRAGRANT MOSSY WOODLAND BASKET

TIME INVOLVED

1 hour

Tools & Materials

Piece of cardboard or sheet
of newspaper

18-in (45-cm) square of
green sheet moss, or the
equivalent in smaller pieces

4-fl-oz (118-ml) bottle
of white glue

Plastic container or bowl

Small foam paintbrush,
1 or 2 in wide (2.5–5cm)

3-in-wide (7.6-cm)
papier-mâché basket or any
woven basket

Scissors

2 lengths of 16-in (40-cm)
raffia or ribbon (optional)

$\mathscr{M}$AKE MOSS BASKETS IN MANY DIFFERENT SIZES. Fill the small ones with a winter or Christmas potpourri and hang them on your tree as fragrant decorations. Or use them as favors at a holiday dinner or as small gifts for guests. Place a large moss basket beside a fireplace or on a tabletop and fill with scented cones, potpourri, or small wrapped packages.

To enhance the fragrance of the potpourri or scented cones, sprinkle a few drops of essential oils inside the basket.

1 Place cardboard on the work surface, then place the pieces of moss on it. Shake each piece to remove bits of dirt. If there is any bark on the back of the moss, gently pull it off.

2 Study the shapes of the different pieces and determine where to glue them on the basket. Tear a strip of moss wide enough to completely cover the basket handle, inside and out, and long enough to reach from the base of the handle on one side to the base on the other.

3 Pour some glue into a bowl. Brush the glue thickly onto the top, bottom, and sides of the basket handle. Fit the moss strip onto the top of the handle and, using the palms of your hands, press it firmly onto the glued surface. Fold the sides of the moss strip under the handle and press them firmly into place. Make sure that the handle is totally covered with moss.

4 Test fit a piece of moss that will cover part of the interior bottom and one side of the basket, as well as fold over the rim and cover a small section of the exterior. Remove the moss, spread the glue thickly over these areas, and fit the moss back in place. Push it down firmly with your fingers to make sure it adheres well.

5 Continue the sequence of selecting, fitting, and gluing the moss until the entire basket is covered. Push the moss down firmly with your fingers to make sure it adheres to these surface areas. If it doesn't, lift up the loose section, dab in extra glue, and press it firmly back into place. Where pieces of moss join, push them together so that the ragged edges of the torn moss will blend into each other, leaving no visible seams. Fill in any bare spots with bits of glued moss. Allow the basket to dry overnight.

6 If you wish, tie bows of raffia or ribbon on either side of the handle where it joins the basket.

To keep the moss from fraying at the edges of the basket, where it is subject to the most wear and tear, always fold the pieces over the edges. This precaution ensures that the butting, or joining, of pieces occurs at less stressful points.

CAMBRIA CHRISTMAS GARLANDS

*D*ECORATE A FESTIVE HOLIDAY TABLE with this beautiful, long-lasting garland. Use it alone or lay it on a flat bed of fragrant fresh evergreens. Try tucking twinkling votive candles in glass cups around the outside edge of the arrangement, or sprinkle gilded pinecones and nuts over the greens.

TIME INVOLVED

2 hours

Tools & Materials

9 x 26-in (23 x 65-cm) piece
of chicken wire

9 x 11-in (23 x 27.5-cm)
piece of cardboard or
sheet of newspaper

6 oz (180g) green
sheet moss

1 thin 3-in (7.6-cm) nail

Quick-drying glue

12 pipe cleaners, 12 in
(30cm) long

White glue

Small dish

Florist's scissors

1 roll ½-in (13-mm) green
or brown florist's tape

2 yd (1.8m) raffia

Botanicals

12 small pomegranates

About 150 long California bay leaves

21 dried red roses

48 red globe amaranths

21 cinnamon sticks, 4 in (10cm) long

15 sprigs of 6-in (15-cm) fresh rosemary

1 Lay the chicken wire flat on a work surface covered with cardboard or newspaper. Arrange the pieces of sheet moss in a rectangular shape, 4 x 24 in (10 x 60cm), down the center of the chicken wire.

2 Fold the bottom third of the chicken wire over the moss and press it flat. Fold the top third of the wire down over the moss and press it into place to form a 3 x 25-in (7.6 x 62-cm) chicken-wire package.

3 Bend the cut ends of the chicken wire to form little hooks that can catch in the mesh holes in the back of the package. Bury the sharp ends in the moss.

4 With a thin nail, punch a hole in the base of each pomegranate.

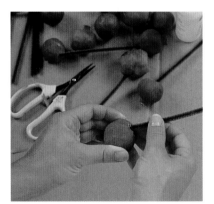

5 Pour some quick-drying glue into the 12 pomegranate holes, and insert a pipe cleaner stem into each. Set aside to dry.

6 Begin outlining the garland base with the California bay leaves. Dip the stems of individual bay leaves into white glue and push them into the moss around the right border of the garland base. Make sure that each leaf lies flat and points to the right.

7 Fill in the top right half of the moss frame with bay leaves that have been dipped in glue. These must also face right, but allow them to curl up toward you in order to create a three-dimensional effect. Turn the moss frame 180 degrees, and glue the rest of the bay leaves to the other half of the frame. When you are finished, all the leaves on the right half of the frame should flow to the right; all the leaves on the left side of the frame should flow to the left.

8 Divide the roses into seven groups, each containing three flowers. Cut the stems to measure 4 in (10cm). Wrap the stems of each group together with florist's tape to make seven bunches.

9 Divide the globe amaranth into 10 groups, each containing three flowers. Cut the stems to measure 4 in (10cm). Tape the stems of each group together with florist's tape to make 10 bunches. Likewise, divide the pomegranates into six bunches of two each, and tape the pipe cleaners of each pair of pomegranates tightly together.

10 Lay the garland base horizontally on the work surface. Place one bunch of pomegranates at the left end of the base; a second bunch toward the center of the left half; one bunch at the right edge; and another toward the center of the right half of the garland. (Reserve one bunch for decorating the center of the garland, and place the sixth bunch wherever you choose.) Then carefully push the taped stem of each pomegranate bunch through the sheet moss and chicken wire. Make sure the fruit is in its proper place, and secure each stem by twisting it back through the chicken wire.

11 Dip the taped stem of each rose bunch into the glue and randomly tuck three bunches into the moss between the curly bay leaves on each side of the garland. Reserve the seventh bunch. Dip the taped stems of each globe amaranth bunch into the glue and push the stems of five bunches randomly into the moss on each side of the garland. Dip the base of each cinnamon stick into the glue and position the sticks at an angle between the bay leaves, roses, globe amaranths, and pomegranates. Dip the bases of the rosemary sprigs into the glue and insert them randomly.

12 With the raffia, make a simple layered florist's bow (page 81) with 4-in (10-cm) streamers, and tie it to the center of the garland. Add the reserved pomegranate and rose bunches to the center so that they nestle against the bow. Let the garland dry overnight.

HERBAL BED PILLOWS

TIME INVOLVED
1 hour

Tools & Materials

2 pieces of lightweight
fabric, 8 x 8 in (20 x 20cm),
washed and ironed

Sewing machine

2 pieces of cotton batting,
7 x 7 in (18 x 18cm)

Iron

1½ oz (45g) herbal mix

Needle and thread

Sharp sewing scissors

If you travel a lot, take an herb pillow with you. It will help you relax during long plane or automobile rides or at bedtime if you are staying away from home.

MALL, FLAT PILLOWS FILLED WITH FRAGRANT DRIED HERBS, flowers, and spices have been used for hundreds of years to enhance sleep, soothe ruffled emotions, and induce sweet dreams. Tuck one inside a pillowcase or place it directly on your bed. The weight and warmth of your hand or head resting on the pillow will help release its subtle, natural fragrances.

Although hops were the most common ingredient in old herbal bed-pillow recipes, today they are rarely included because of their unpleasant, acrid odor. Mixtures containing roses, lavender, rosemary, various mints, dill, sage, pine needles, and thyme have become very popular. Try English Farmhouse (page 66), with its clean, refreshing scent, or Mind's Ease (page 39), with its rich rose perfume.

Before making an herb pillow, wash, dry, and iron the fabric for the outside bag. Sizings, soil, excess dye, or pesticide residue on the fabric surface could affect the herbal fragrances.

CAUTION!
Use herbal blends, not potpourris, for bed pillows. The latter often contain orrisroot and fragrance oils, which can cause strong allergic reactions in some people. In fact, if you suffer from allergies, it is essential to know all the herbal ingredients used in the filling.

STEP-BY-STEP

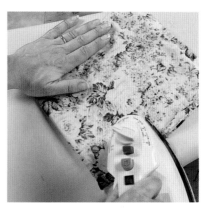

1 Place the two pieces of fabric together, wrong side out, and machine-stitch around three sides.

2 Place the two pieces of cotton batting together and sew around three sides, leaving the fourth side open.

3 Fold the raw edges of the opening ¼ in (6mm) over the fabric bag and press. Turn the bag right side out.

4 Carefully fill the cotton-batting pillow with the herbal mix, and machine-stitch the fourth side closed.

5 Insert the cotton-batting pillow into the fabric bag, easing it into the corners.

6 Hand-sew the opening closed. Cut the thread from the spool and securely knot.

ROMANTIC ROSEBUD HEARTS

TIME INVOLVED
30 minutes

Tools & Materials

12 in (30cm) 24- or
26-gauge florist's wire

24–26 small rosebuds
(either mauve rosebuds
or freeze-dried
miniature roses)

2 pieces of ⅛-inch-wide
(3-mm) 10-in-long
(25-cm) satin ribbon

Quick-drying craft glue

Small dish

Sharp scissors

Sheet of paper or
newspaper

3 or 4 whole boxwood
or uva-ursi leaves

3–4 puffs of baby's breath,
½ in (13mm) long

*S*IMPLE TO MAKE, ROMANTIC ROSEBUD HEARTS can be used to add a charming touch to wedding, engagement, or anniversary packages, to give as favors on Valentine's Day, or to make a tiny, meaningful present for a special friend. In the latter case, you might want to sprinkle some rose potpourri on the bottom of the gift box before placing the hearts inside.

The hearts are also ideal for decorating gift bags of wedding herbs, a bottle of champagne, or to use as napkin rings for a bridal luncheon.

*M*ake a ½-inch (1.3-cm) right-angled hook at one end of the florist's wire to prevent the rosebuds from sliding off while you string them.

STEP-BY-STEP

1 Thread the wire through the center of a rosebud from side to side, pushing the bud all the way to the hooked end. String the rest of the rosebuds onto the wire, reserving one rosebud for the final decoration. (The number of rosebuds you need depends on their size.)

2 Carefully twist the two ends of the wire together and gently shape the string of rosebuds into a heart. The spot where the wires join becomes the center of the heart.

3 To decorate the heart and hide the ends of the twisted wire, tie a two-loop, two-tail bow with a piece of the satin ribbon. Pour some glue into a small dish. Lay the heart on a sheet of paper and attach the bow to the top of it with a dab of glue.

4 Snip off any bit of stem remaining on the reserved rosebud. Coat the base of the rosebud with glue, then push it into the center of the bow.

5 When the rosebud is dry, dip the stem ends of the boxwood or uva-ursi leaves into the glue and tuck them around the rosebud. Glue on a few puffs of baby's breath over the boxwood leaves.

6 Tie the remaining piece of satin ribbon to the heart to make a loop for hanging.

SUMMER MEMORIES GERANIUM WREATH

TIME INVOLVED
1½ hours

Tools & Materials

Straw wreath or crimped wire ring, 8 in (20cm) in diameter

1 spool of waxed green florist's twine or heavy green carpet thread

Sharp scissors

2 lbs fresh scented geranium leaves on short stems

*S*CENTED GERANIUMS, WHETHER PLANTED IN A GARDEN OR POT, produce an abundance of scented green leaves during their growing season. A wreath provides a soul-satisfying way to use this fragrant wealth before it is cut down by winter's chill or severely pruned to prepare the plant for a winter greenhouse.

A glass hurricane lamp surrounded by this scented wreath makes a lovely centerpiece for the late summer and early fall. To add a festive accent at Thanksgiving, twine some bittersweet berries and a few dried flowers through the wreath. At Christmas, decorate it with pinecones, ribbons, and boxwood. When you are ready to replace the wreath, don't throw it away. Strip off the geranium leaves, place them in a washcloth, and tie it together with a rubber band. Toss this sachet into a dryer and your garments will be scented with one of summer's best fragrances.

1 Lay wreath form flat on work surface. Tie the free end of the spool of florist's twine firmly onto the wreath form. Cut off the geranium leaves from their heavy central stems, keeping a 1½-in (3.8-cm) stem on each leaf. (Dry the central stems and use them for scent in the fireplace.)

2 Make a cluster of four or five different kinds of geranium leaves, bunching the short leaf stems tightly together. Lay the cluster against the inside of the wreath base, with the stems pointing to the spot where you tied on the twine. Bind the stems securely to the wreath form with the twine.

3 Make another cluster of leaves. Place it snugly beside the first and bind it tightly to the wreath form. Keep the wreath flat on the work surface while adding each cluster of leaves. This helps to create an even shape.

4 Place the third cluster beside the second and bind it firmly to the wreath form. Now a thick ruffle of green leaves completely covers one part of the form.

5 After binding the first three bunches, position the fourth cluster of leaves on top of the stems of the first bunch, completely hiding them. (The fourth bunch of leaves begins a second row of plant material.) Continue covering the form by binding each new cluster of geranium leaves over the stems of the preceding cluster.

6 Once the form is covered with fragrant green leaves, tie off the spool of twine. Use the wreath immediately, or lay it on a flat-woven mat or basket to dry. To protect its color and fragrance, keep it out of direct sunlight and away from high humidity.

Plant material shrinks as it dries, so be prepared to add extra bunches or half bunches of leaves in order to fill spaces left by the drying process.

TINY FRAGRANT WREATHS

T HESE MINIATURE WREATHS MAKE EXCELLENT GIFTS or decorations. Make one for a friend or make a dozen to decorate your Christmas tree.

TIME INVOLVED
30 minutes

Tools & Materials

12 in (30cm) 20- or 22-gauge florist's wire

1 roll ½-in (13-mm) green or brown florist's tape

½-in (13-mm) straight pin

1 spool of transparent nylon thread

15 in (38cm) ¼-in-wide (6-mm) satin ribbon or lightweight satin cording

Small bottle of white glue

Small, shallow dish

Sharp scissors

Botanicals

6-in-long (15-cm) strip of scented green sheet moss, about ½ in (13mm) wide, or the equivalent in small pieces

Assortment of tiny to small dried flowers, leaves, and seedpods

Scented pinecones

STEP-BY-STEP

1 Make the base following the directions for the Mother's Herb Wreath (pages 126–27), but use scented sheet moss (see page 120) instead of plain. Once the wreath base is finished, tie a satin ribbon around it and adjust the tails so that they are even in length. Tie these together at the top of the base to form a loop for hanging.

2 Pour some glue into a shallow dish and set out individual piles of assorted plant material. Glue a double layer of plant material, such as annual statice pieces, around the top of the wreath base. Make sure each piece is slightly angled, so that the ruffled tips peek over the edge of the mossy base. This arrangement gives the wreath a lacy look.

3 Evenly space bunches of three or six larger flowers, such as roses, strawflowers, or globe amaranths, around the wreath, then glue them on. To cover any gaps, as well as to increase visual interest, decorate with fern tips, boxwood clusters, baby's breath, and other attractive plant material. Allow the wreath to dry for at least 1 hour.

I t's easier to dip the backs of flowers and tips of leaves into glue than to squeeze the glue onto the plant material.

$\mathscr{H}$ere are the materials to use for three popular varieties of tiny, fragrant wreaths:

Pinecone & Pepperberry Wreath
white statice
pink pepperberries
red cockscomb
tiny pinecones
gilded eucalyptus pods
boxwood sprigs

Rose, Juniper & Tallow Berry Wreath
white statice
roses
cranberries
juniper berries
tallow berries
gilded eucalyptus berries
green boxwood leaves
gilded boxwood leaves

Strawflower Wreath
strawflowers
yarrow
Australian daisies
boxwood leaves

WOODLAND TWIG BALL AND SCENTED STAR

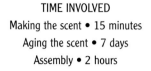ANG SEVERAL FRAGRANT DECORATED BALLS AND TWIG STARS of varying sizes in a window at different levels to create a beautiful and fragrant woodland scene at Christmas. If the balls or twigs begin to lose their scent, drip some fresh fragrant oil into the moss.

TIME INVOLVED
Making the scent • 15 minutes
Aging the scent • 7 days
Assembly • 2 hours

Tools & Materials

1-quart (.95-l) glass jar with a tight-fitting lid

Eyedropper

4- or 6-in (10- or 15-cm) twig ball

White glue

Small dish

1-in (2.5-cm) paintbrush

2 pieces of raffia, 6 in (15cm) long

2 pieces of ½-in-wide (13-mm), 6-in-long (15-cm) gold ribbon

Raffia and gold ribbon multiloop figure-8 florist's bow (page 81)

Cardboard or sheet of newspaper

4- or 6-in (10- or 15-cm) twig star

2½ ft (75cm) raffia, for bow

2½ ft (75cm) of ½-in-wide (13-mm) gold ribbon, for bow

Botanicals

2 oz (60g) green sheet moss, for ball

¼ oz (7g) sheet moss, for star

½ oz (14g) gray Spanish moss

30 rosehips

10 clusters of ½-in (13-mm) pink pepperberries

Oils

8 drops fir needle oil

4 drops juniper oil

10 drops balsam oil

TO CREATE THE SCENT

Shake out the sheet moss to remove any dirt or bits of bark, and pack the sheet moss into a quart-sized (.95-l) jar.
Use an eyedropper to carefully drip the fir needle, juniper, and balsam oils, a drop at a time, onto the moss.
Cap the jar tightly and shake vigorously.

TO AGE THE SCENT

Allow the oiled moss to mature for 7 days.

Twig balls are available at most craft shops in different sizes. If you can't find green sheet moss, you may substitute Spanish moss for the interior of your twig ball.

STEP-BY-STEP Twig Ball

1 Gently poke a finger into the center of the twig ball, pushing aside the twigs to make a small pocket or cavity. Carefully stuff it with half the scented sheet moss. Push the twigs back together.

2 Tear the rest of the sheet moss into small strips. Pour a small amount of glue into the dish. With a brush, dab some glue onto the back of the torn pieces and randomly press them onto the surface of the ball. Don't cover all the twigs. Try to create the impression that the moss has grown naturally on the ball.

3 Place ¼ oz (7g) of the gray Spanish moss on the work surface. Pinch off small clumps of the moss, dip into the glue, and press onto the twig ball. Randomly glue five clusters of three rosehips each and five clusters of pepperberries to the sheet moss.

4 Pull the short lengths of raffia and gold ribbon under a sturdy twig at the top of the ball.

5 Center the multiloop figure-8 florist's bow on top of the same sturdy twig. Tie the raffia and gold ribbon around the center of the bow. To enhance the scent, you can drip 10–12 drops of fragrance oils onto the moss before hanging it.

STEP-BY-STEP Scented Star

1 Place the cardboard over the work surface. Lay the twig star on it. Pour a small amount of glue into the dish. Tear the scented sheet moss into thin, trailing pieces. Beginning in the center and working out toward the points, spread the glue thickly onto a twig, using a paintbrush. Then press a strip of sheet moss onto the twig.

2 Place ¼ oz (7g) of gray Spanish moss onto the work surface. Pinch a small amount of the moss between your thumb and forefinger and dip the base of it into the glue. Press this small clump onto a piece of glued sheet moss. Glue several more small clumps of Spanish moss randomly onto the pieces of sheet moss.

Don't completely cover the twigs, as they are as pretty as the moss and provide a rich contrast to it.

3 One by one, dip the base of five clusters of pepperberries into the glue and arrange them on top of the sheet moss. Follow the same procedure with five clusters of three rose hips each. Allow the star to lie flat to dry on the cardboard for an hour.

4 To hang the twig star, run a strand of raffia and gold ribbon through one of the points on the star. Tie it together at the top to form a loop. If you wish, drip some fragrant oil onto the moss before hanging it.

HERBAL BATH SCRUB

TIME INVOLVED

30 minutes

Tools & Materials

3 oz (90g) unscented soap

Food grater

Large glass, stainless steel, pottery, or enamel mixing bowl

12 oz (340g) old-fashioned oatmeal

6 oz (180g) herbal mix, such as English Farmhouse (page 66)

Stainless steel spoon

Decorative jar or canister with a tight-fitting lid

Plain washcloth

Heavy string or decorative cord

*H*ERBAL FRAGRANCES CAN BE STIMULATING OR SOOTHING. Try this aromatic bath scrub in your shower or bath, and your spirits will be refreshed, your body cleaned, and the bathroom filled with a lovely, lingering scent. When the soap stops bubbling through the washcloth, remove the tie and discard the used-up blend. Just refill the washcloth and it is ready to use again!

For a relaxing bath at the end of the day, substitute 6 oz (180g) equal parts lavender flowers, hops, rose geranium leaves, and chamomile flowers for the English Farmhouse (page 66) botanical blend.

Herbal bath scrubs make wonderful presents, especially during these hectic times. Arrange them in a gift box and don't forget to include a package of blend for refills.

STEP-BY-STEP

1 Grate the soap into a large mixing bowl, pressing against the grate with long strokes.

2 Add the oatmeal and the herbal mix and stir gently with a stainless steel spoon.

3 Store the soap blend in an attractive covered jar or canister in the bathroom. To use, scoop 4 or 5 Tbsp (60 or 75g) into the center of a plain washcloth.

4 Gather all the edges of the washcloth around the soap blend and tie with heavy string or decorative cord to make a foaming bath scrubber.

MOTHER'S HERB WREATH

TIME INVOLVED
1 hour

Tools & Materials

12 in (30cm) 22- or
24-gauge florist's wire

1 roll ½-in-wide (13-mm)
green or brown
florist's tape

1 spool transparent
nylon thread

½-in (13-mm) straight pin

Sharp scissors

White glue

Small dish

Botanicals
*All botanicals (except moss)
are either clusters of leaves or
flowers on single stems or
individual flower heads*

6-in-long (15-cm) strip
of green sheet moss, about
½ in (13mm) wide, or the
equivalent in
small pieces

3 hawthorn clusters

3 rose flowers

3 larkspur clusters,
blue or white

3 carnation flowers

3 blue salvia flowers

3 feverfew clusters

7 heartsease flowers

3 globe amaranth flowers

3 thyme clusters

3 marjoram clusters

3 boxwood clusters

3 artemisia clusters

*S*URPRISE YOUR MOTHER ON HER BIRTHDAY or Mother's Day with this beautiful and symbolic floral offering.

1 Bend the florist's wire into a circle 3½ in (9cm) in diameter. Twist the overlapping ends of the wire around the circle.

2 Bind the circle with florist's tape, pulling and stretching the tape to achieve a smooth, continuous covering for the circle.

3 Tie the free end of a spool of transparent nylon thread onto the base. Lay a piece of sheet moss over the knot in the thread and begin rolling the spool of thread.

Keep the spool tight against the frame and the thread taut as you roll it around the moss. Continue to add more moss in the same manner until the circle is evenly covered and bound to the frame.

4 Finish binding by twisting some thread several times around the straight pin. Push pin into moss, then cut the thread.

STEP-BY-STEP Decorating the Base

1 Arrange the flowers and herbs in groups. Study the colors and textures of your materials and think about the pattern you want to create. Choose one group of flowers or herbs, such as roses. Snip off their stems.

2 Dip the base of each flower into the glue. Gather them in clusters and attach to the circle. Continue gluing clusters of plant material. Allow the wreath to dry in place for at least an hour before you handle it.

TINY TRAVEL SACHETS

TIME INVOLVED

30 minutes

Tools & Materials

Potpourri

Rolling pin or hammer

6 empty tea bags

Set of stainless steel measuring spoons

Large-eyed sewing needle

Embroidery thread

Sewing scissors

6 lengths of ⅛-in-wide (3-mm), 7-in-long (18-cm) ribbon

ILL DOZENS OF THESE TINY SACHETS WITH DIFFERENT POTPOURRIS. Color-code the bags by choosing thread and ribbon colors that complement the scent of each mix, such as green for New Zealand Pinewood (page 71) or yellow for Luscious Lemon (page 74). Then stack and tie an assortment of bags together, like a pile of pillows, and give them to your friends. Be sure to include a card reminding the recipient not to use them as tea bags! These pretty little packets are handy for adding a pleasing scent to pocketbooks, wallets, desk drawers, books, suitcases, and briefcases.

STEP-BY-STEP

1 If your chosen potpourri has large pieces in it, crush them lightly with a rolling pin or hammer. If you don't, the large pieces are likely to tear the fragile tea bags.

2 Carefully spoon 1 level Tbsp (15g) of the potpourri into each bag.

Purchase empty tea bags from an herb shop or mail-order source. The bags are open on one side.

3 Thread a large-eyed sewing needle with colorful embroidery thread and stitch the open side closed.

4 Fold a 7-in (18-cm) piece of narrow ribbon into a simple figure-8 bow (page 81) and hand-stitch it to the bag.

The following recipes make wonderfully fragrant filling for the Tiny Travel Sachets:

Revive! *(page 44)*

Catalpa Plantation Herb Garden *(page 43)*

Last Rose of Summer *(page 59)*

Lavender House Rose Garden *(page 42)*

Pennyroyal Rose *(page 56)*

LIST OF BOTANICALS

Red Zinnia
Zinnia elegans
and
Baby's Breath
Gypsophilia paniculata

Common Name	Scientific Name
Acorns	*Quercus robur*
Acrocliniums	*Helipterum roseum*
Alder cones	*Alnus spp.*
Allspice berries	*Pimenta dioica*
Angel wings	*Oroxylum indicium*
Annual statice	*Limonium sinuatum*
Apple	*Malus spp.*
Apple mint	*Mentha rotundifolia*
Artemisia, White sage	*Artemisia ludoviciana 'Silver King'*
Baby's breath	*Gypsophilia paniculata*
Balsam fir	*Abies balsamea*
Basil	*Ocimum basilicum*
Basket flower	*Centaurea spp.*
Bearberry, Uva-ursi	*Arctostaphylos uva-ursi*
Bee balm	*Monarda didyma*
Bells of Ireland, Shellflower	*Moluccella laevis*
Blueberries	*Vaccinium spp.*
Blue cornflower, Bachelor's button	*Centaurea cyanus*
Blue gum, spiral	*Eucalyptus globulus*
Boxwood	*Buxus sempervirens*
California laurel, California bay	*Umbellularia californica*
Cape jasmine, Gardenia	*Gardenia jasminoides*
Cardamom seed	*Elettaria cardamomum*
Carnation	*Dianthus caryophyllus*
Cedar	*Cedrus spp.*
Cedronella	*Cedronella triphylla*
Celery leaf	*Apium graveolens*
Cellulose granules (ground corncob)	*Zea mays*
Ceylon cinnamon quills	*Cinnamomum zeylanicum*
Chili pepper	*Capsicum annuum*
Chrysanthemum	*Chrysanthemum spp.*
Cinnamon	*Cinnamomum cassia*
Citrus	*Citrus spp.*
Cloves	*Syzygium aromaticum*
Cockscomb	*Celosia cristata*
Coriander	*Coriandrum sativum*
Cranberries	*Vaccinium macrocarpom*
Dark opal basil	*Ocimum basilicum purpureum*
Delphinium	*Delphinium*
Dill	*Anethum graveolens*
Drumstick allium	*Allium sphaerocephalon*
English hawthorn	*Crataegus laevigata*
English lavender	*Lavandula angustifolia*
Eucalyptus	*Eucalyptus spp.*
European white birch bark and cones	*Betula pendula*
Fennel	*Foeniculum vulgare*
Feverfew	*Chrysanthemum parthenium*

Common Name	Scientific Name
Field poppy flowers, Red poppy flowers	*Papaver rhoeas*
Frankincense tears	*Boswellia carteri*
Garden sage	*Salvia officinalis*
Garlic	*Allium sativum*
German chamomile	*Matricaria chamomilla*
German statice	*Limonium dumosa*
Ginger	*Zingiber officinale*
Globe amaranth	*Gomphrena globosa*
Golden yarrow	*Achillea filipendulina*
Grains of paradise	*Aframomium melegueta*
Grapefruit	*Citrus paradisi*
Gum benzoin, Snowbells	*Styrax spp.*
Heartsease	*Viola tricolor*
Hemlock cones	*Tsuga canadensis*
Hibiscus pods	*Hibiscus*
Hickory nut shells	*Carya ovata*
Honesty, Money plant, Silver dollars	*Lunaria annua*
Hops	*Humulus lupulus*
Hydrangea flowers	*Hydrangea macrophylla*
Juniper	*Juniperus communis*
Lady's-mantle flowers	*Alchemilla vulgaris*
Larch cones	*Larix*
Larkspur	*Consolida regalis*
Lemon	*Citrus limon*
Lemon balm	*Melissa officinalis*
Lemon geranium	*Pelargonium crispum*
Lemongrass	*Cymbopogon citratus*
Lemon Leaf	*Oaultheria*
Lemon thyme	*Thymus x citriodorus*
Lemon verbena	*Aloysia triphylla*
Lime	*Citrus aurantiifolia*
Mealycup sage, Blue salvia	*Salvia farinacea*
Mint	*Mentha spp.*
Mock orange blossoms	*Philadelphus*
Moss	*Mniumhoenum*
Mugwort	*Artemisia vulgaris*
Myrrh	*Cistus creticus*
Myrtle	*Myrtus communis*
Nigella, Love-in-a-mist	*Nigella damascena*
Nutmeg	*Myristica fragrans*
Oak leaves	*Quercus robur*
Oakmoss	*Evernia prunastri*
Orange	*Citrus sinensis*
Orrisroot	*Iris germanica*
Patchouli	*Pogostemon cablin*
Pearly everlasting	*Anaphalis margaritacea*
Peony	*Paeonia officinalis*

Purple coneflower
Echinacea purpurea

LIST OF BOTANICALS

Teasel
Dipsacus fullonum spp.

Common Name	Scientific Name
Peppermint	*Mentha piperita*
Perennial chamomile	*Chamaemelum nobile*
Pine needles and cones	*Pinus spp.*
Pink pepperberries	*Schinuf terebinthifolius*
Pomegranate	*Punica granatum*
Pot marigold	*Calendula officinalis*
Purple coneflower	*Echinacea purpurea*
Red cedar	*Juniperus virginiana*
Red sandalwood	*Pterocarpus santalinus*
Rose	*Rosa spp.*
Rose hips	*Rosa spp.*
Rosemary	*Rosmarinus officinalis*
Rose-scented geranium	*Pelargonium graveolens*
Rue pods	*Ruta graveolens*
Safflower	*Carthamus tinctorius*
Sandalwood	*Santalum freycetiarum*
Sheet moss	*Hypnum curvifolium*
Southernwood	*Artemisia abrotanum*
Spearmint	*Mentha spicata*
Spruce needles	*Picea abies*
Star anise	*Illicium verum*
Strawflower	*Helichrysum bracteatum*
Sumac berries	*Rhus glabra*
Sunflower petals	*Helianthus annuus*
Sweet bay, Laurel	*Laurus nobilis*
Sweet flag, Calamus root	*Acorus calamus*
Sweet gum balls	*Liquidambar styraciflua*
Sweet marjoram	*Origanum majorana*
Sweet woodruff	*Galium odoratum*
Tallow berries	*Myrica cerifera*
Tangerine	*Citrus reticulata*
Tansy	*Tanacetum vulgare*
Teasel	*Dipsacus fullonum spp.*
Thyme	*Thymus vulgaris*
Tilia star flowers	*Ternstroemia spp.*
Tonka bean	*Dipteryx odorata*
Vanilla bean	*Vanilla planifolia*
Vetiver	*Vetiveria zizanioides*
Wild vanilla, Deertongue	*Trilisa odoratissima*
Winged everlasting	*Ammobium alatum*
Wormwood	*Artemisia absinthium*
Yarrow, Sneezewort	*Achillea ptarmica 'The Pearl'*
Yellow sandalwood	*Santalum album*
Zinnia	*Zinnia elegans*

CONTRIBUTORS

United States

Susan Adam
Adams Garden of Eden
360 North Anguilla Road
Pawcatuck, CT 06379
Revive! (page 44)

Susan Bassetti
Green Valley Flower Company
P.O. Box 4
Harmony, CA 93435
California Moonlight (page 38)
Cambria Christmas (page 70)
Cambria Christmas Garlands
(page 108)

Clara Berger
Harvest Thyme
7415 State Road
Cincinnati, OH 45230
Fragrant Mossy Woodland Basket
(page 106)

Sue Brungs
The Old Greenhouse
1415 Devils Backbone Road
Cincinnati, OH 45233
Summer Memories Geranium Wreath
(page 116)

Marge Clark
Thyme Cookbooks
Route 1, Box 69
West Lebanon, IN 47991
Oak Hill Farm Christmas (page 40)
Luscious Lemon (page 74)

Carol Huettner
27 Hazel Street
Manheim, PA 17545
Scented Beads and Ornaments
(page 84)

Arlene Kestner
Good Scents of Louisiana
11655 Highland Road
Baton Rouge, LA 70810
Mind's Ease (page 39)

Theresa Neff Loe
Country Thyme Productions
P.O. Box 3090
El Segundo, CA 90245
Orange Peel Heart Wreath (page 82)

Jim Long
Long Creek Herbs
Route 4, Box 730
Oak Grove, AR 72660
Long Creek Holiday Greens (page 64)

Sharon Lovejoy
Heart's Ease
4101 Burton Drive
Cambria, CA 93428
From a California Garden (page 62)

Maryland Massey
Maryland's Herb Basket
399 Hazel Lane
P.O. Box 131
Millington, MD 21651
Holiday Greens (page 53)
Maryland's Colonial Rose (page 73)

R.M. Nichols McGee
Nichols Garden Nursery
1190 North Pacific Highway
Albany, OR 97321-4580
Last Rose of Summer (page 59)

Theresa Mieseler
Shady Acres Herb Farm
7815 Highway 212
Chaska, MN 55318
Minnesota Harvest Moon (page 75)

Constance N. Miller
Green Horizon Farm Herb Shop
100 Guy's Lane
Bloomsburg, PA 17815
Green Horizons Christmas (page 72)

Jackie Pike
Texas Nature Treasures
5615 Woodcrest
Fort Worth, TX 76140
Texas Christmas (page 68)
Simply Friends (page 48)

Mary Preus
Silver Bay Herb Farm
9151 Tracyton
Bremerton, WA 98310
Silver Bay Citrus (page 50)

Linda Quintana
Wonderland Tea & Spice Herb Shop
1305 Railroad Avenue
Bellingham, WA 98225
Cascade Robe Guard (page 47)
Muslin Moth Bags (page 100)

Patricia Reppert
Shale Hill Farm
6856 Hommelville Road
Saugerties, NY 12477
Woodland Walk (page 76)
Woodland Twig Ball and Scented Star
(page 120)

Susanna Reppert
Rosemary House and Gardens
120 South Market Street
Mechanicsburg, PA 17055
Herbal Bath Scrub (page 124)

Maureen Rogers
Herb Growers and Marketing Network
P.O. Box 245
Silver Spring, PA 17575
Lust (page 52)

Renae Smith
Catalpa Plantation
2295 Old Poplar Road
Newman, GA 30263
Catalpa Plantation Herb Garden
(page 43)

Barbara L. Wade
Herb 'n' Ewe
11755 National Road SE
Thornville, OH 43076
November on the National Road
(page 54)

CONTRIBUTORS

Australia
Di Waters
Pennyroyal Herb Farm
Penny's Lane
Branyan, Bundaberg 4670
Australia
Pennyroyal Rose (page 56)

Carol White
Lavandula Lavender Farm
Newstead Road
Hepburn Springs
Victoria, Australia 3461
Blue Heaven (page 67)

Japan
Akiko Kumai
6-23-17 Jindaiji Higashimac
Chofu-shi, Tokyo, Japan
Chrysanthemum Festival (page 58)

England
Caroline Moss
Lavender House Press
445 Lode Lane
Solihyll West Midlands
England B92 8NS
Lavender House Rose Garden (page 42)

Nina Pagan
Elly Hill Herbs
Elly Hill House
Brampton
Darlington
Co. Durham DL1 3JF England
English Farmhouse (page 66)

Canada
Lynda Dowling
Happy Valley Herbs
3497 Happy Valley Road
Victoria, BC V9C 2YC Canada
Vancouver's Summer Song (page 57)
Happy Valley Evening Song (page 60)

Cindy Elliott-Theberge
Trouvez
2237 Chemin des Patriotes
Richelieu, Quebec J3L 4A7
Canada
Peony (page 46)

New Zealand
Olive Dunn
Floresta Fragrant Garden
86 Chelmsford Street
Invercargill, New Zealand
New Zealand Pinewood (page 71)

Carmel Hare
Aroha Cottage Herb Garden
Jesmond Road RD2
Drury, New Zealand
Aroha Cottage Citrus Zest (page 45)

United States

Alloway Gardens and Herb Farm
456 Mud College Road
Littlestown, PA 17340
717-359-4548
717-359-4363
lavenders (a specialty)

Best of Thyme Herbs
P.O. Box 534
Mt. Gretna, PA 17064
717-964-3503
dried citrus, dried apples

Frontier Herbs
3021 78th Street
Norway, IA 52318
800-669-3275
botanicals, oils, craft supplies

Gilberties Herb Gardens
7 Sylvan Lane
Westport, CT 06880
203-227-4175
oils

The Glass Pantry
231 Cherry Alley
Maysville, KY 41056
bottles of all shapes and sizes

Good Scents of Louisiana
11655 Highland Road
Baton Rouge, LA 70810
504-766-3898
504-767-0061 (fax)
botanicals, oils

Green Valley Flower Company
P.O. Box 4
Harmony, CA 93435
*botanicals, oils, fresh-cut herbs,
freeze-dried flowers*

The Herb Farm
32804 ISS-Fall City Road
Fall City, WA 98024
800-866-4372
botanicals, oils

Home-Sew
P.O. Box 4099
Bethlehem, PA 18018-0099
610-867-3833
*lace by the yard, ribbon roses,
hard-to-find treasures*

Lavender Lane
5715 Donerail Drive
Sacramento, CA 95842
916-334-4400
916-339-0842 (fax)
bottles, tea bags, oils

Lewis Mountain Herbs & Everlastings
2345 S.R. 247
Manchester, OH 45144
513-549-2484
513-549-2886 (fax)
botanicals, freeze-dried herbs and flowers

Nature's Herb Company
1010 46th Street
Emeryville, CA 94608
510-601-0700
botanicals, oils

Nichols Garden Nursery
1190 North Pacific Highway
Albany, OR 97321-4580
503-928-9280
503-967-8406 (fax)
botanicals, oils

Paine Products
Kittyhawk Avenue
P.O. Box 1056
Auburn, ME 04211-1056
balsam, cedar

Penzeys Ltd. Spice House
P.O. Box 1448
Waukesha, WI 53187
414-574-0277
spices and other botanicals

SOURCES OF POTPOURRI SUPPLIES

Rosemary House and Gardens
120 South Market Street
Mechanicsburg, PA 17055
717-697-6111
botanicals, books, oils

Shady Acres Herb Farm
7815 Highway 212
Chaska, MN 55318
612-466-3391
612-466-4739 (fax)
oils, botanicals, fixatives

Shale Hill Farm and Herb Gardens
134 Hommelville Road
Saugerties, NY 12477
914-246-3429
914-246-6982 (fax)
books, craft supplies, oils

Spice Caravan
45 Carmine Street
Suite 1D
New York, NY 10014
212-633-1380
212-691-7234 (fax)
Moroccan herbs, fruits, flowers

Sunburst Bottle Company
7001 Sunburst Way
Citrus Heights, CA 95621
916-722-4632
*decorative and cobalt blue bottles,
plastic bottles, jars, tea bags*

Tom Thumb Workshops
P.O. Box 357
Mappsville, VA 23407
804-824-3507
botanicals, oils

Village Herb Shop
152 South Main Street
Chagrin Falls, OH 44022
216-247-5014
*botanicals, oils, potpourri,
tussie-mussie supplies*

Wonderland Tea & Spice Herb Shop
1305 Railroad Avenue
Bellingham, WA 98225
360-733-0517
botanicals, oils

Wood Violet Books
3814 Sun Hill Drive
Madison, WI 53704
608-837-7207
books, herbal crafts, herbal gardening

Australia
Australian Botanical Products
39 Melverton Drive
Hallam, Victoria 3803
03-796-4833
03-796-4966 (fax)
botanicals, oils

The Fragrant Garden
Portsmouth Road
Ernia 2250
043-67-7322
043-65-1979 (fax)
botanicals, oils

Fragrant Herb Cottage
Corner of Lemke & Roghan Roads
Taigum, Queensland 4034
07-3216-2422
07-3216-2453 (fax)
botanicals, oils

Honeysuckle Cottage
Lot 35 Bowen Mountain Road
Bowen Mountain, NSW 2753
045-721-345
botanicals, oils

Lavandula Lavender Farm
Newstead Road
Hepburn Springs, Victoria 3461
botanicals, oils

Canada

Happy Valley Herbs
3497 Happy Valley Road
Victoria, BC V9C 24Z
604-474-5767
botanicals, lavender (a specialty)

Magnolia's
Box 220
Zephyr, Ontario L0E 1T0
905-473-8703
800-663-4785
botanicals, oils

Richter's
357 Highway 47
Goodwood, Ontario L0C 1A0
905-640-6677
905-640-6641 (fax)
E-mail: catalog@richters.com
botanicals, oils, plants

Trouvez
2237 Chemin des Patriotes
Richelieu, Quebec J3L 4A7
514-658-7311
botanicals, oils, roses (a specialty)

England

Culpeper Ltd.
21 Burton Square
London W1X 7DA
0171-629-4559
botanicals, oils, plants

Hambledon Herbs
Court Farm
Milverton, Somerset TA4 1N7
018-23-401-205
botanicals, tea bags

Neal's Yard (mail order)
5 Golden Croft
Cornmarket Street
Oxford OX1 3EU
018-65-245-436
botanicals, oils

Neal's Yard (main store)
Covent Garden
15 Neal's Yard
London WC2 H9DP
0171-379-7222
botanicals, oils

Willow Herb
139 Claremont Road
Rugby, Warwickshire CV21 3LU
017-88-540-749
oils

New Zealand

Arthur Holmes Ltd.
P.O. Box 368
Newtown, Wellington
04-389-4103
bottles, jars, eyedroppers

Bronson & Jacobs
10 Flower Street
Eden Terrace, Auckland
09-309-2528
essential oils

Crombie & Price Ltd.
P.O. Box 121
Oamaru
containers

Dragonspace
11 Mount Eden Road
Eden Terrace, Auckland
09-357-0753
dried herbs, essential oils, gums, resins

King's Herb Heaven
P.O. Box 19004
Avondale, Auckland
09-828-7588
botanicals, craft supplies, oils

BIBLIOGRAPHY

Black, Penny. *The Book of Potpourri.* New York: Simon & Schuster, 1989.

Bremness, Lesley, ed. *Herbs.* Pleasantville, NY: Reader's Digest, 1990.

Clarkson, Rosetta E. *Herbs: Their Culture and Uses.* New York: Macmillan, 1942.

Duff, Gail. *Natural Fragrances: Outdoor Scents for Indoor Uses.* Pownal, VT: Storey Communications, 1989.

Farwell, Edith F. *A Book of Herbs.* Fredonia, NY: White Pine Press, 1979.

Fettner, Ann T. *Potpourri, Incense and Other Fragrant Concoctions.* New York: Workman Publishing, 1977.

Fischer-Rizzi, Susanne. *Complete Aromatherapy Handbook.* New York: Sterling Publishing, 1989.

Fletcher, Kim. *Essential Oils.* New York: Viking Penguin, 1995.

Foster, Maureen. *The Flower Arranger's Encyclopedia of Preserving and Drying.* New York: Sterling Publishing, 1988.

Garland, Sarah. *The Complete Book of Herbs and Spices.* New York: Viking Press, 1979.

Genders, Roy. *The Cottage Garden and the Old-Fashioned Flowers.* London: Pelham Books, 1969.

Gips, Kathleen M. *The Language of Flowers: A Book of Victorian Floral Sentiments.* Chagrin Falls, OH: Pine Creek Herbs, 1990.

Gips, Kathleen M., ed. *Scented Geraniums: A Herbal Handbook.* Cleveland: Herb Society of America, 1989.

Greenaway, Kate. *The Language of Flowers.* New York: Frederick Warne, 1977.

Gruenberg, Louise. *Potpourri.* Norway, IA: Frontier Cooperative Herbs, 1984.

Herb Society of America. *Herbs for Use and for Delight.* New York: Dover, 1974.

Hylton, William H. *The Rodale Herb Book.* Emmaus, PA: Rodale Press, 1974.

Jekyll, Gertrude. *Home and Garden.* London: Longmans Green, 1900.

Joosten, Titia. *Flower Drying with a Microwave.* Asheville, NC: Altamont Press, 1988.

Juniper, Sunny, and Dylan W. Davis. "On the Scent of a Real Rose." London: *The Herbal Review,* Winter 1988.

Kowalchik, Claire, and William H. Hylton, eds. *Rodale's Illustrated Encyclopedia of Herbs.* Emmaus, PA: Rodale Press, 1987.

Laufer, Geraldine A. *Tussie Mussies.* New York: Workman Publishing, 1994.

Lyness, Dody. *Potpourri . . . Easy as One, Two, Three!* Rancho Palos Verdes, CA: Berry Hill Press, 1982.

BIBLIOGRAPHY

Magic and Medicine of Plants. Pleasantville, NY: Reader's Digest, 1986.

Meares, Portia. "A Fragrance Garden: New Zealand's Gentle Climate Nurtures a Wonderland." Loveland, CO: *The Herb Companion*, December 1994/January 1995.

Ohrbach, Barbara M. *The Scented Room.* New York: Clarkson N. Potter, 1986.

Plat, Sir Hugh. *Delightes for Ladies.* London: Crosby Lockwood & Son, 1948.

Rohde, Eleanour S. *A Garden of Herbs.* Boston: Hale, Cusman and Flint, 1936.

Rohde, Eleanour S. *Herbs and Herb Gardening.* New York: Macmillan, 1937.

Romanne-James, C. *Herb Lore for Housewives.* London: Herbert Jenkins, 1938.

Scourse, Nicolette. *The Victorians and Their Flowers.* Beaverton, OR: Timber Press, 1983.

Shaudys, Phyllis V. *Herbal Treasures.* Pownal, VT: Storey Communications, 1990.

Shaudys, Phyllis V. *The Pleasure of Herbs.* Pownal, VT: Storey Communications, 1987.

Siegler, Madeleine H. *Making Potpourri.* Pownal, VT: Storey/Garden Way Publishing Bulletin A-130, 1991.

Silber, Mark, and Terry Silber. *The Complete Book of Everlasting.* New York: Alfred A. Knopf, 1988.

Simmons, Adelma G. *Herb Gardening in Five Seasons.* New York: Hawthorn Books, 1964.

Stuart, Malcolm, ed. *The Encyclopedia of Herbs and Herbalism.* New York: Crescent Books, 1974.

Tolley, Emelie, and Chris Mead. *Herbs.* New York: Clarkson N. Potter, 1985.

Tucker, Arthur O. "The Ancient Memories of Perfume," "Fragrance Old and New," "Some Things Never Change." Loveland, CO: *The Herb Companion*, December 1994/January 1995.

Verey, Rosemary. *The Scented Garden.* New York: Van Nostrand Reinhold, 1981.

Webster, Helen N. *Herbs: How to Grow Them and How to Use Them.* Boston: Ralph T. Hale, 1939.

Wilder, Louise B. *The Fragrant Garden: A Book About Sweet Scented Flowers and Leaves.* New York: Dover, 1974.

SUGGESTED READING

Austin, David. *English Roses,* 1993. Little, Brown, Boston, MA.
ISBN 0-316-05975-7.

Cottage Garden Society. *The Cottage Gardener's Companion,* 1993. David & Charles, Newton Abbott, Devon TQ12 4PU, England. ISBN 0-7153-0020-2.

Denman, Carol M. *Cooking and Crafting with Herbs and Flowers,* 1992. Wild Geranium Studio, Route 55A, Box 681, Napanoch, NY 12458.

Dowling, Lynda. *Herbal Adventures,* 1995. Westside Inst-A-Print, 2811 Jacklin Road, Victoria, BC V9B 3X8, Canada.

Druit, Liz, and G. Michael Shoup. *Landscaping with Antique Roses,* 1992. Taunton Press, 63 South Main Street, Box 5506, Newton, CT 06470-5506.
ISBN 0-942391-64-0.

James, Tina. *Lovely Lavender: A Fragrant Collection of Recipes, Folklore and Gardening Advice,* 1990. Alloway Gardens Print Productions, 256 Mud College Road, Littlestown, PA 17340.

Lacey, Stephen. *Scent in Your Garden,* 1991. Little, Brown, Boston, MA.
LC No. 91-52504.

Oster, Maggie. *Gifts and Crafts from the Garden,* 1988. Rodale Press, Emmaus, PA.
ISBN 0-87857-775-0.

Reppert, Bertha. *Herbs for Weddings and Other Celebrations,* 1993. Storey Communications, Schoolhouse Road, Pownal, VT 05261.

Sheen, Joanna. *Herbal Gifts,* 1992. Ward Lock, Villiers House, 41/47 Strand, London WC2N 5JE, England. ISBN 0-304-34272-6.

Tolley, Emelie, and Chris Mead. *Gifts From the Herb Garden,* 1991. Clarkson Potter Publishers, 201 East 50th Street, New York, NY 10022. ISBN 0-517-5762-0.